SEXUALITY
SUMMARY

- Have there REALLY been developments in sexual morality?
- On what information can you now "form your conscience"?
- Has the "anything goes" principle become respectable?
- Are your views too broad-minded — too strict?

The questions are endless and the answers are scattered over thousands of magazine articles not readily available to the average reader.

This highly-practical book brings questions and answers together. May it shed a ray of light on this important area of your life.

William F. Allen

SEXUALITY SUMMARY

ALBA ▲BOOKS

NIHIL OBSTAT

James A. Clarke

Reverend James A. Clarke
Vice Chancellor

IMPRIMATUR

James W. Malone

The Most Reverend James W. Malone
Bishop of Youngstown

January 3, 1977

Library of Congress Catalog Card No. 76-47357

ISBN — 0 — 8189 — 1141 — 7

Printed in the United States of America

CONTENTS

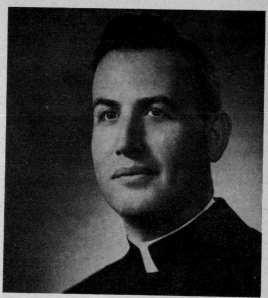

THE AUTHOR

Father William F. Allen took his Philosophy in the Grand Seminarie of Montreal and his Theology at St. Sulpice, Paris. After a year's parish ministry he began studies in the Rome Lateran University where he received his Doctorate in Canon Law.

He taught Moral Theology and Canon Law at St. Bernard's Seminary, Rochester, N.Y., and later was Instructor in Ethics, Psychology and Religion in the St. Luke's School of Nursing, Springfield, Massachusetts. For the past twenty-five years he has been a regular contributor to the principal American and English clergy magazines meantime carrying on regular parish ministry and doing also a great deal of work in the social and mental health areas.

PREFACE

Many talk today about a sexual revolution that has taken place in the last twenty years. Others see in this same phenomenon a period of progress from which we have obtained a deeper and finer understanding of the sex drive. Even in religious thought we have come to a better appreciation of the content and the role of human sexuality in human fulfillment.

If we are to grasp the correct orientation of human sexuality it is imperative that we have a clear notion of what is meant by these words. In our time, they are so often taken as a synonym for genital, erotic pleasure whereas they refer to an all-embracing expression of human affection. We are so wrapped up in pansexualism that we reduce every expression of love, even the highest and most spiritual, to a response of the sexual libido. Every loving friendship of compassion, concern, warmth and sensitivity is classified as a purely sexual manifestation. Marc Oraison writes that (in human sexuality) we are concerned with a basic, very general, emotive energy... psychological in the wide sense of which the genital aspect is only the culminating and so to speak, specialized manifestation. The point to which this energy may lead emotionally will depend upon the person's intensity of feeling and the circumstances of a given situation.

Bishop Mugavero looks upon it as a quality of personhood which enables us to enter into loving relationships with others. It is a relational power of person to person whence flow the qualities of understanding, sensitivity, warmth, openness and mutual respect. It may express itself in the purest, most altruistic fashion all the way down to the dominance of the physical and passionate in the partnership of conjugal love. But in whatever form, there is always a giving of self either in the degree of friendship or concern, or in agape, the perfect sharing in a spiritual sense, or in the sharing with another motivated by the desire of self-gratification through intimacy in which body, emotions, passion and imagination all play a vital part in erotic love. In whatever degree, human sexuality is noble for it must always contain a gift of self if it is to be genuine and true.

In most controversies it is the genital aspect of human sexuality that is primary and the principle that is most in question concerning human sexuality is this: sex is essentially procreative.

It is essentially a social dimension even if secondarily it has personal benefits. There has been a change in the manner of conceiving sex on this score. Depth psychology has influenced thought to the extent that greater sexual freedom is claimed as essential to one's personal development and for personal enrichment; sex is the language of relationship, intimacy, communication. The social aspect of sex has been given a low profile whilst the existential aspect is now of the utmost concern.

Vatican II in its Decree "The Church in the Modern World," follows this mentality in depicting marriage as an intimate partnership of love, stemming from a conjugal covenant based on irrevocable consent whereby the spouses initiate a community of life by the mutual gift of self to one another. This community makes them two in one flesh, leads to mutual help and service and ultimately prepares them for a family vocation which includes children. The emphasis is on communion of life.

The Roman Rota had this mentality in its latest decisions. One Judge wrote "conjugal life ... most especially consists in a intra-personal relationship underlying which in both parties is a healthy intra-personal balance and integration; if this is lacking in one or both, then such parties can be judged unable rightly to understand the true meaning of the communion of life, called 'marriage,' which is for the procreation and education of children." There is a giving of self on the part of both, that is the basis for this com-

munion of life and love and the ultimate perfection of which will be fatherhood and mother-
hood.

Such a very personal concept of what marriage is to the modern world, has appealed im-
mensely to our contemporaries. Once they feel
this communion of life, this gift of self verified
in their companionship, they claim the right to
marry regardless of their juridical capacity. So
we have a wave of pre-marital sex and extra-
marital sex and we have divorced Catholics pleading for the right to a second marriage on the
grounds that their prior valid marriage was not
one of communion of life and love: they truly
had never given the gift of self therein.

It is only by means of a sex-friendship-service
covenant, permanent and exclusive, that a true,
loving, unselfish, human intimacy arises. It is
only in this situation that there is truly sexual
complementarity and perfectibility on all levels,
biological, spiritual and emotional. It is only thus
that two persons really feel and live their need
for each other as persons and, in living this
personal need, permit their love to develop, not
into a plaything of erotic pleasure, but into an
instrument of begetting flesh of their flesh, an
image of their love and of themselves.

Today three trends challenge this doctrine
of the nature of human sexuality. People need
to love; spouses need one another as persons
for perfection on all levels of human development, but *homosexuality* seeks a selfish love
with no possibility of human perfectibility on all

levels; *contraception* denies that perfection to the spouses; *abortion* effectively ends the development once it has infringed on the freedom of the spouses or the parties to the joys of human sexuality. The pages which follow outline the main ideas to be kept in mind in considering these trends.

PART I

HOMOSEXUALITY

We might define homosexuality as a psycho-sexual attraction to members of the same sex. It is a sexual bias or propensity constituting the *major* sex drive, since in the same person there may be a minor, heterosexual drive. Dr. John Cavanagh defines it a little more amply: "overt homosexuality is a permanent state in which the sexual object is a person of the same sex and in which there is a concomitant aversion or abhorrence in varying degrees to sexual objects and contacts with members of the other sex." He goes on to say that "latent homosexuality refers to the same condition but in this case, it exists outside the patient's consciousness." We must not go as far as thinking that homosexuality is a state or condition on a par with heterosexuality since in the same individual there could be a sex drive of variable quantitative strength from exclusive homosexuality to apparent exclusive heterosexuality.[1]

Some contend that the sex component could have been genetically constituted, or could just be the product of early environmental factors.

Some contend that the sex component could also have been acquired in later life due to external factors such as abnormal segregation. One must be careful to distinguish between the homosexual *condition* and homosexual *acts*. It is very possible that the sex component could incline to occasional irregular practices and actions, but the chaste homosexual could well control himself and avoid both. On the other hand, another person might well have overt deviate actions but still not have a major propensity to these in his sex urge and thus would not be numbered among the homosexuals by condition. The real, practicing homosexual would have frequent actions of a nature and strength indicative of a basic, only-to-males erotic attraction. It is estimated that in our country 4% of the adult male population, and 1% of the adult females are exclusively homosexuals whilst 30% of the adult males, and 25% of the females have had at least one homosexual encounter. Thus, one group is homosexual by condition, whilst the others are not really of the homosexual condition but are open to deviate actions.[2]

ENVIRONMENTAL FACTORS

Family upbringing is very important in the development of homosexuality. The very early years are crucial to the future of the child. Some hold that the child is sex-oriented at the age of five. Dr. Irving Bieber insists that "we have come to the conclusion that a constructive, supportive, warmly-related father precludes the possibility of a homosexual son (and for that matter a lesbian daughter); he acts as a neutralizing protective agent should the mother make seductive or close-binding attempts." A common trait of deviates is loneliness; they seem to have a feeling that they do not belong; they long for affection. This should have been given in the family circle. Lacking this family warmth, the potential homosexual may meet a male who will answer this need and awaken deep emotional impressions and yearnings of male to male. We cannot over-stress the importance of a loving, sexually-adjusted home foyer.

PARENT RELATIONSHIPS

Various psychological and also environmental causes may be found in the home atmosphere which fosters the potential deviate. The boy hungering for affection meets a male who emotionally fulfills his yearnings. A boy abandoned by his father identifies with his mother emotionally; or vice versa for the lesbian. The male parent may be too liberal and give bad example to his offspring in this sense of irresponsible use of sex. There may be faulty sex education; puritanical views of sex; attitudes of promiscuity lived and urged by parents. A dominant mother or an over-protective one who makes the boy a "mama's boy" or one who wanted a daughter and treats the boy as a girl as a substitute for her own satisfaction — this sort of maternal conduct is one of the most common causes of homosexuality.

An over-athletic father who prods his unwilling son to athletic prowess may drive the boy to hate all demonstrations of physical strength and glorification of manliness. It is evident that a certain type of personality and temperament with a deviate potential factor which comes in contact with these environmental influences can easily become prey to overt homosexuality. How much importance is to be attributed to environment in this regard? It is difficult to give an accurate evaluation since much depends on the emotional structure of the persons involved. This accounts for the fact that many confirmed homosexuals have come from the healthiest heterosexual milieux and many normal heterosexuals are relatively unharmed by the most advanced type of homosexual environment.[3]

SEDUCTION

Over 90% of the homosexual cases start by seduction and yet experts hold that the sex initiation is generally the occasion and not the cause of the ensuing homosexuality dominance! It is the passing-into-act and consciousness of an already, pre-existing, perhaps subconscious propensity. The worst seduction is Infanto-homosexual practice. It is a very complicated case of abnormal sex satisfaction by a sick personality whose mental age will be about the same as the youth seduced. The evil consequences of this seduction must be kept to a minimum by careful psychological treatment, and the interested parties must not communicate their emotional abhorrence to the victim in too heavy emotional tones. Homosexual initiation between adults is much less harmful since the parties are better able to deal with the experience from an emotional viewpoint.

UNNATURAL SEGREGATION

Perhaps the most blatant homosexual initiation takes place in prisons and correctional institutes due to the boredom, depressing outlook, loneliness, and low moral standards of the system. Rejected by society, living in overcrowded cells, subjected to continuous sex-references in conversation, prisoners find homosexual practices attractive. Sometimes compliance by the victims gives them a pass to the underworld of vice and material rewards. Again, it is the emotional danger of segregation in prisons and correctional institutions that must be stressed as the environmental factor, not the cause.

Close friendships between older and younger boys may be the occasion of sex initiation and sex deviations. This happens in all-boys boarding schools. Worthy of note is the comment of one author in this regard. The person involved in this kind of sex initiation is often one who has used religion or sublimation or repression to check his need for sex expression. He has always feared a psychic eruption of sexual perversion to satisfy his pent-up feelings and "the ones most likely to find themselves in trouble with the law are the pious, strong-minded men who have established themselves in the community." Experience teaches this truth.[4]

THE JUDEO-CHRISTIAN VIEWPOINT

In the Judaeo-Christian constant tradition, homosexual practices have been considered seriously sinful and unequivocally condemned. The Sodom and Gormorrah incident in Gen. 19 verses 4-11 had great influence on this score. The question is asked: was it homosexuality that caused the two cities to be destroyed by God? The crowd demanded that Lot produce his two angelic visitors that the Sodomites might "know" them. Lot tried to persuade the crowd to be content with his two daughters and to abuse them instead of the visitors. Though the crowd was not to win its point, God visited the cities with dire punishment.

The argument is over the word "know." The hebrew word used, *yadha* is "to know" in the sense of "engaging into action with," and can have other meanings. But in the Old Testament it is used eleven times expressly with the meaning of "coition." In Judges 19, *yadha* signifies "homosexual abuse" and the Jerusalem Bible uses it for "sexual abuse." The Sainte Bible in France accepts the same meaning. The Interpreter's Bible says "the men of the city demanded that Lot hand over his guests to them that they might gratify their unnatural lust."

Some scholars maintain that the word *yadha* in the above text meant simply that the crowd wanted information on the visitors and that, if it desired them homosexually, then the word *shakhabh* would have been used. This word is used mostly for sinful coitus as in the case of rape and abuse. But the angels could not sin, so the word would have been out of place in this text. It would seem that the choice of *yadha* was correct and had a homosexual meaning, according to the common consensus of scriptural scholars.

Tradition attached a severe stigma to homosexual acts because of the utter destruction visited on Sodom and Gormorrah for the magnitude and scandal of their sin. "And the Lord said that the cry of Sodom is multiplied and their sin has become exceedingly grievous" (Gen. 18, v. 20). Equal punishment was implied for all who would imitate the Sodomites. (Cf. Gen. 13, v. 13, 18, v. 20; Jer. 23, v. 14, Wz 14, v. 49; Jude 7). For this reason, the Fathers of the Church were all vehement in their denunciation of the sin of homosexuality. Clement of Alexandria, St. John Chrysostom, St. Augustine, the Apostolic Constitutions, are all of the same mind. Augustine wrote "those shameful acts such as were committed in Sodom ought everywhere, and always, to be detested and punished. If all nations were to do such things, they would be equally held guilty of the same crime by the law of God which has not made that men should use one another in this way." (Conf. III, 8, PL 32, 689). The early councils of Elvira (305), or Ancrya (314), of Naples (1120), the Lateran in 1179 and all the Penitentials speak of the heinous sin and condemn it. St. Thomas in the Summa (II-II, Q. cliv. ad 4) writes against sodomy as *contra naturam* and an insult to the Creator.

There has been no change in the Church's attitude to homosexual practices up to the present, as is evidenced by the most recent instruction on this subject from the Sacred Congregation for the Doctrine of the Faith, Dec. 29, 1975, entitled "The Vatican Declaration on Sexual Ethics." In paragraph 8 of this document we read "it (Scripture) does attest to the fact that homosexual acts are intrinsically disordered and can in no case be approved of." Heterosexuality is considered as the only sexual state; homosexuality has never been considered as an inter-sex state but rather as a bad-habit fixation, in most instances. The Church could not teach otherwise for in the same document paragraph 5 we read "This same principle, which the church holds from divine revelation, and from her authentic interpretation of the natural law, is also the basis of her traditional doctrine, which states that the use of the sexual function has its true meaning and moral rectitude only in true marriage."

In the Christian dispensation, it is St. Paul who teaches the sanctity of our bodies since they are temples of the Holy Spirit and he violently attacks homosexuality in both male and female (cf. Rom. I, vv. 24-27; in I Cor. 6, v. 10, and I Tim. 1, v. 10). Formal condemnation of homosexual actions can be found in Leo IX's Letter *Ad splendidum nitentis* (1054), in the Decree of the Holy Office, March 2, 1679; in the Allocutio of Pius XII, Oct. 8, 1953 and in "The Church in the Modern World," no. 51 (if we place it in the general category of masturbation with special aggravating circumstances).[1]

THE MEDICAL VIEWPOINT

How does the homosexual condition happen? It is known that the sex drive originates in the hypothalamus section of the brain but what causes it to be male-oriented, or female-swayed is not that certain. The human embryo is bisexual up to the sixth week of development and contains male and female structures in an undeveloped state. Normally, if the genetic constitution is male, the testes will begin to produce small amounts of testosterone, the main sex hormone, which in turn will cause the female structure to degenerate and the hypothalamus to become male. The production of male hormones escalates and the embryo is definitely male. Both sexes produce male and female sex hormones known as androgens and estrogens. The degree of masculinity or femininity of the male or female will depend on the ratio of A to E and thus wide variations can occur.

It is very probable that an imbalance of sex hormones plus environmental factors could well account for a great deal of male homosexuality and lesbianism. It is not a modern phenomenon, since some historians find homosexuality among the primitive tribes as well as in the very ancient and cultured civilizations. In fact, the name Lesbian comes from the isle of Lesbos in the Aegean and was given to the action in the 6th century B.C.

CHROMOSOMES — HORMONES

Those who contend that the condition is due to organic causes lay the blame on the chromosomes or the hormones. Those who think chromosomes are responsible claim that the male is a woman in disguise and that his genetic sex does not agree with his physical body-build. Others blame an imbalance in the hormones: the male has a female hormonal system with the consequent sexual direction and urges of the female. The ductless glands are presumed to play a dominant role in the homosexual propensity as well as in the appearance of secondary female characteristics (or male in the case of lesbians).

We cannot deny that some sex deviates have secondary physical traits of the opposite sex: some males are effeminate in their physique, and some females have male traits. But it is not possible to correlate body-build and the incidence of homosexuality. On the contrary, it is admitted that as a group, homosexuals are very virile, and lesbians very feminine in their physical aspect.

Their body build, compared to heterosexuals as a group, is only slightly different and could not form the basis of an intersex between the male and the female. The average measurements of the body of the male homosexual are closer to the male norm than to the female. Homosexuality due to a genetic basis is implied in only a small minority of cases and cannot be scientifically proven to have universal application.

Could the hormonal theory base at least a predisposition to homosexuality? A British doctor, Sawyer, researched the question and found that sex behavior in the two sexes develops so differently that it could not be the direct result of the production of sex hormones. Males have a tremendous upsurge of sex ability at puberty while females have a slow increase with steady growth up to about 30. It would seem that sexual responsiveness depends more on psychological conditioning and availability of sex outlets than on the circulation of hormones. Furthermore, the use of hormones in the cure of homosexuality has been very disappointing; this would lead one to conclude that hormones do not play that important a role in the deviation. The secondary sex characteristics do come from an excess of hormones of one sex or the other, but this excess does not determine the person to homosexuality and neither do the secondary sex traits. Medical men know of only one type of homosexuality that responds to hormonal treatment and that is the physically-determined eunuchoidal, passive deviate. Logically, we may conclude that genetic aberrations and endocrine disorders possibly may dispose to homosexuality but they do not cause it. Environment is needed for them to declare themselves. Dr. Morris Fisbein wrote "in other words the training is the differential in the individual's ultimate behavior." [1]

To assess correctly the subjective imputability of homosexual practices we must be clear as to the origin of homosexuality in any one particular instance. Medical science sees no conclusive proof that the deviation is an innate, organic-constituted condition, except perhaps for the eunuchoidal, passive type. That it is a biological or endocrinological state cannot be asserted because of lack of sufficient medical proofs. There is no evidence that it is a pathological condition and it is fairly well accepted that the causative factors are not purely medical or physical.

It could well become a psychiatric disorder as a result of the emotional strain and conflict set up by the homosexuality propensity. But in psychiatric practice the idea of a constitutive homosexual that is to say, that the person is permanently oriented in that direction is not universally accepted. Recently, an author wrote "I would like to call your attention to the fact that the American Psychiatric Association not only supports the notion that homosexuality per se implies NO impairment in judgment, stability, social or vocational capability, but further urges psychologists to take the lead in removing the stigma that has long been associated with homosexual orientation."

There may be a PHYSICAL propensity-basis (either hormonal or chromosomal) which was encouraged by various environmental factors (particularly home atmosphere or early childhood) and which the person himself or herself fixed more or less permanently by emotional responses of positive or negative nature. We might call this process "bad-habit fixation." Some insist that the person may have reacted positively to the propensity so long and vehemently that he or she may come to the point of being quasi organically constituted in the deviate condition i.e., irreversible, fixed in homosexual outlook and practices. The recent Vatican declaration on sexual ethics seems to envisage this case.

If the deviation is to be placed in the "bad-habit fixation" category then there is possible responsibility for its origin. Authors describe the homosexual condition as an emotional disaster with roots going back to childhood and a natural propensity. This gives rise to a false concept of human love which in turn goes uncorrected and is strengthened by interior and exterior actions; in this way it becomes the dominant sex drive and the willing accomplice of concupiscence. With no effort made to control the instinctive movements of the senses, a habitual reaction arises which colors every decision; a certain compulsion to act in a homosexual manner takes shape when passion beckons, and the emotional and spiritual life of the victim is overwhelmed by the deviation. The reaction of the person to this psychological state will give some inkling of his responsibility for the actions that spring from it.[2]

Face to face with the propensity, the person has three choices: he or she may have the will to change and become heterosexual whatever the cost in terms of a long struggle. He may feel it impossible to change and give in to a fatalism which suggests that for him to be other than he is, amounts to fantasy. Or, he may turn to a narcissistic type of reaction and regress to indulging in self-centeredness and seek a David-and-Jonathan relationship of love with the soul who loves him in the same manner. Happiness for him is in a homosexual setting. The practising homosexual has a false concept of love "for him the discovery will be to find himself in another being; his joy will be to recognize in another his own reflection scarcely altered; his security finally will consist in being able to read in his partner . . . the answer already anticipated . . . an echo of his question."[3]

Though he may seek only the love of friendship, love without genital sex, such liasons usually culminate at that level of passion. At the outset there may be no conscious intent of seeking homosexual practices, but sooner or later the mutual expression of affection will involve just this kind of love. In almost every case history we read the sad message "each time I fall in love with a man I really only want him as a friend. I really do not know why I have to go and spoil it all." This is the deep sadness of all those who give in to homosexual practices: they are doomed to be emotionally unbalanced and profoundly unhappy.

Why? It is not the fear of detection, nor of society's disapproval, nor even a sense of guilt. Experts believe that "it is inherent in the nature of an activity for which the bodily organs employed are physically unsuited." If the origin of homosexual practices is indeed a misadventure, the ending is doubly so even in the seemingly successful deviate life.

THE MORAL VIEWPOINT

Given all this background, it is very difficult to offer a practical norm whereby to measure moral imputability. There is a truism that no homosexual is one because he wishes to be one. It all starts with a propensity of mysterious origin that is permitted to grow consciously or unconsciously through environmental factors so that it becomes a dominant factor in the sex urge and the practices end up as bad habits rooted in one's makeup. The first source of moral fault is the subject's failure to correct the bad habit before it becomes seriously ingrained. The second source is the victim's willing acceptance of the deviate state with a fatalistic mentality and a desire to seek sexual fulfillment in a homosexual manner within certain limits, or within no limits whatever. We are presuming that outside of a psychotic condition, the person is not generally incurable nor without some control of the homosexual condition.

However gravely sinful homosexuality is in itself, it is very likely NOT gravely sinful from a subjective viewpoint, namely in the mind of the afflicted. Usually the person discovers that he is a homosexual; he has not willed, nor sought this moral deviation. Rarely can he change his sexual orientation unless this is done in his early years. His responsibility before God for his actions will depend on the degree of freedom which the person possesses in the control of his deviate orientation.

How much responsibility is present? The extreme left would be the true compulsive homosexual with little or no control. He is practically irreversible. The extreme right would be the person who has as much control over his urges as the heterosexual. One is inclined to see a certain degree of compulsiveness in every deviate and so the real problem, moral as well as physical and psychical, is NOT the strength of the sexurge but rather the individual's ability to adjust to the tension within his own personality stemming from the aberration. Rarely can we say that the subject has no freedom to resist. But very often his freedom is so diminished that his *voluntary* actions are weakened.

Dr. Allers would maintain that the homosexual labors under a neurosis of a compulsive nature which centers around a false, adolescent-type concept of human love. It is conceived as a love-communion of souls. This bespeaks a disorder of the total person and strangely enough, it will be the depth of this personal disorder and not the sex drive, that will give strength to the compulsion. Once this neurosis, or fixed idea (sex with same sex) is activated, it is susceptible of reaching a high degree of tension until satiety is obtained in full passion. The author would affirm that the person feels capable of stopping the progressive development of the evil act but will not do so under tension and this is the basis for his partial moral responsibility. It seems that one is justified in assessing responsibility for the acceptance of the bad habit, and for pursuing sexual satisfaction in that manner and certainly there is conscious advertence and premeditation especially when the homosexual acts involve another. Despite all attempts to establish norms of moral fault in concrete cases it must be remembered that no "all or none" judgment is possible. Each case must be considered on its own merits once we are agreed that in all cases, with very few exceptions, there is some degree of liberty and free will in play.[1]

The most recent declaration from the Vatican, reasons along the same lines. It castigates those who would judge very indulgently and even completely excuse homosexual relations, and this for the category of incurables (par. 8). The document seems to classify homosexuals in those open to rehabilitation and cure and those who are not. The former are victims of environmental factors such as false sex education, bad example, bad habit formation; the other class is incurable because the propensity has developed into a quasi pathological condition or is due to an "innate instinct" and is considered a permanent condition.

We are admonished to treat all classes with understanding, and sustain them in the hope of overcoming their personal difficulties and their inability to fit into society. Their culpability will be judged with prudence but at the same time no method can be countenanced that would consider such acts as morally justified simply because they are consonant with the condition of homosexuals. Objectively, homosexual actions are condemned in Scripture as a serious depravity and it attests to the fact that such actions are intrinsically disordered and may in no case be approved. By the same token we cannot conclude that all who are so afflicted are personally responsible for this condition.

Those who deal with both types of deviates must follow the normal procedures for eradicating a bad habit with much tact and understanding, especially with the incurable type, bordering on the irreversible. Their long range goal will be to lead them back to as near a normal level as is possible, all things considered, both in their emotional and their sex life. The immediate task is to try to reinforce their control of the propensity, by getting them to know their psycho-sexual setup, the "how" of the condition, and the manner in which the urge is enticed by its object.

Hope must be held out to all, and to the transient or to those not permanently fixed in the condition, assurance must be given that this abnormality can be overcome. Naturally, complete abstinence from all homosexual activity will be very disturbing emotionally and sexually and should there be relapses one must ascribe them to weakness rather than to malice. This difficult period will continue until the person has found a new way of life that will be both satisfying and purposeful: a life that will give him acceptance, friendship, affection and recognition of his own person and its virtues, values and talents; a life that may bring him even soul-companionship.

In personal counseling sessions such persons should be catechized to a greater love and knowledge of God. Through a life of prayer, sacramental grace, modern methods of meditation for self study and orientation, they should be brought to a confrontation with their weakness as is done in drug rehabilitation programs. Group therapy would be most useful to awaken a desire to success and to instill confidence that success is possible. With the slightest indication of good will and effort at making occasions of sin remote, even if this is unsuccessful, we should encourage participation in the Sacrament of Reconciliation and the Eucharist.

Many say that the first step for the curable deviate must be to renounce his condition as the only one for him and the only possible source of sex fulfillment. Gradually, he must get to this goal since without it, sucess will be very problematical. He must be convinced and desire that the condition be controlled to that extent. If he comes to the point of desiring the heterosexual condition the possibility of genuine reform is assured especially if he seeks the companionship of the other sex and ceases frequenting places for deviate associations. If the person cannot bring himself to desire the heterosexual condition because of fear, or of inadequacy, success is still attainable if he aims at the control of the tendency, especially when under passion and violent temptation. With personal counseling, group therapy, religious instruction, religious practice and a routine of daily life based on diminishing the strength of the propensity, there is every possibility that such a person can live a happy, Christ-like life. The struggle may not definitively end but it will have its reward in a sense of interior peace.

THE LEGAL VIEWPOINT

It is frequently said that the Law should not attempt to control private morality, and very many are agitating for the legislation of homosexual actions between consenting adults. In fact, many courts take a very lenient attitude toward cases of this type. Following the admonition of the Church to be compassionate toward these deviates, it would not be out of order for those wishing to help to come to the aid of the homosexuals once in trouble and to procure legal aid for them. We should not sympathize with entrapment policies and vigilante practices in their regard and should work to have a calming influence on the community if reactions run high when homosexuality is discovered. Yet we can hardly be adverse to corrective measures if the deviate is guilty of seduction, especially of children or even unwilling adults. His crime should not be ascribed to an "abnormal" person. The homosexual is not to be classified as a criminal set apart from other criminals.

The treatment of sexual offenders is notoriously deficient in our own country. Institutions for the treatment and management of such offenders are hard to come by. We may have sufficient knowledge as to what is best for their proper development but to get the ideal conditions under which to apply that knowledge as well as the funds necessary and the willingness of the Courts and civil powers to cooperate to that end is still a dream. Punishment has no effect on this type of offender and excessively long sentences tend to aggravate their condition, yet some limitation of their freedom looms necessary. Most states at the present time refer them temporarily to mental institutions where some form of special treatment is administered even though it may be seriously inadequate according to psychiatric standards.

Since it is not easy to predict repetitive behavior in this area, the public vehemently criticizes their release when their antisocial behavior is repeated. The public should ascribe the repeated bad behavior to the effect of inadequate treatment originally administered. It is the "whole" person that must be treated from every angle. The cure will not be simply prescribing drugs. It is a problem of control of the malfunctioning sexual urge and the control will come from the will of the deviate. Human sciences as well as religious ideals can contribute to this goal.

In their professions, homosexuals are as successful as heterosexuals and should be left alone unless they offend the community by their overt actions. But even the well-controlled should not seek to teach in an all-boys' school. High government positions are not desirable for homosexuals since, if their deviate actions become known, blackmail might result with the most unfortunate private and public scandals. But we should not espouse the principle that a homosexual should be immediately fired from whatever job or position he holds. The cause of the firing must not be homosexuality in itself: the effects may justify the action if these can be shown as very probable if not actually real.

This is a poignant question when it concerns the dismissal of such a person among the student body: should the deviate be expelled on the pretext of protecting the other students? Would it make a difference were the student in a college, or in the secondary school? We must be realistic enough to recognize that people do have irrational reactions; we should attempt to ameliorate the situation. We must be optimistic enough to believe that most such offenders can be helped and the road to recovery should start with you and me.

In every one of the United States homosexual acts between males is an offense. This does not always apply to females. Illinois exempts from prosecution those males who had previously consented to this exchange of affection. For the most part, such actions are classified as "crimes against nature" and include anal and oral penetration for adults and bestiality. If the actions include assaults against unwilling and non-consenting adults or the molestation of children, the guilty ones are numbered among "sexual psychopaths." Even if most jurists, physicians and social workers are of the mind that between consenting adults these actions should not be brought under criminal headings, such remedial legislation is not yet possible because of the stubborn, emotional opposition of society to any leniency on this score.[1]

OTHER VIEWPOINTS

John J. McNeill, S.J. has published his book
"The Church and the Homosexual" after a two
year tussle with the Censors. It attempts to justify
the moral goodness of homosexual practices.

Gregory Baum, has his own theory favorable to the homosexual. "Dignity" an organization
of gay Catholics affirms "gays can express their
sexuality in a manner that is consonant with
Christ's teachings."

Fr. McNeill contends that the sin for which
God destroyed Sodom was not overt homosexuality but rather that of inhospitality. "It is the myth
of Sodom and Gomorrah . . . that homosexuality is
contrary to the will of God." The Church has
erred, according to McNeill, in her interpretation
of the biblical circumstances which caused the
destruction of the cities and has perpetuated a
structural social injustice against the homosexuals.

He thinks the early Church was prejudiced against the deviates because the Christians looked upon homosexual acts as related to prostitute cults among the Greeks and Romans. St. Paul looked upon the deviate acts in the same light too; for him they were acts of Old Testament idolatry and the Saint says McNeill, was not aware of the distinction between the homosexual condition and the homosexual genital act and this stemmed from a lack of distinction between custom and nature.

Theologians wonder how Fr. McNeill can thus circumvent the plain language of Romans I vv. 26-27 and I Corinthians 6. McNeill would have us look upon the homosexual experience as having been fashioned as a cultural image through which human beings could achieve the fullness of a true personal relationship — an experience of mature human love . . . and any action by a loving person is an unique act not measurable by any extrinsic norm, its morality comes from within the will of the person himself . . .

Gregory Baum looks at cultures in their historical aspects as depicting human nature in various times, and thinks that our rejection of homosexuality is due to a lack of appreciation of the foundations of our culture. Possibly, homosexuality is not against nature given the mores of the times. Jesus never spoke about the subject — what does His silence tell us? All mankind is summoned to true humanism, to become more truly human each day. "If the homosexual can live that kind of life (of love) then homosexual love is not contrary to the human nature." For those who are constitutively homosexual and who allow for the necessary mutuality in their relationship, they should acknowledge themselves before God, accept their calling, and explore the meaning of this inclination for the Christian life.

Fr. Henry Fehren, a priest-professor in the West is quoted in "U.S. Catholic" magazine to the effect that homosexual acts have been condemned as immoral because of a misinterpretation of stray biblical texts written for another age and culture and on a vague unproved natural law .... homosexuals should be free (with no judgment of moral guilt on our part) to satisfy their sex drive and appetite if no harm is done to either party.

Fr. Tom Oddo, C.S.C., speaking at a conference on pastoral counseling, held that there are some gay relationships which are sacred ... where a genuine and deep sense of love exists ... they are beautiful.

In reading these favorable-to-homosexual-acts citations, the words of the Vatican document give the best commentary "at the present time there are those who, basing themselves on observations in the psychological order, have begun to judge indulgently and even to excuse completely homosexual relations between certain people ... they do so in opposition to the constant teaching of the magisterium and to the moral sense of the Christian people." [1]

The same trend showed up at the 1976 meeting of the House of Deputies of the Episcopal Church in Minneapolis, Minn. The assembly affirmed by resolution that "homosexual persons are children of God who have a full and equal claim with all other persons upon the love, acceptance and pastoral concern and care of the church." Local and state governments have been asked to repeal laws against private homosexual acts between consenting adults.

When the debate was over it seemed that many of the delegates wanted the Episcopal Church to declare that homosexual activity is a sin and that the church should be open to deviates who seek forgiveness but that they should not look to the church to give approval to the homosexual life-style. Some in the assembly raised the possibility of homosexuals becoming priests since it is know that one of the women recently ordained a deacon was an avowed lesbian. Evidently, the Scriptural basis for the condemnation of homosexuality is being bypassed, or discarded as an antiquated cultural taboo, and acceptance is being based on sociological and psychological principles. It is vital to recognize progress in the social disciplines but not at the cost of orthodoxy and revealed truth.

Some writers on this subject advocate compromise. When we read of a "compromise solution" we must be aware that the motivation is one of deep pastoral concern which reads the law not in terms of strict legality but with a fine sense of mercy and compassion. As one author tells us: in Moral we are dealing with principles but in pastoral theology we are concerned with persons and the goal of pastoral theology is to obtain the good of the well-disposed individual in his present actual situation. Without doubt, homosexuality practice is intrinsically immoral according to the constant teaching of Scripture and the Church and cannot be approved or recommended in itself.

But, Father Curran of Catholic University writes "My approach for the definitive or irreversible homosexual is based on the theory of compromise which acknowledges that because of his condition, *for which the individual is in no way responsible* (?) (italics mine) these actions are not wrong provided there is a context of loving commitment to another. This does not imply that there are no ethical differences between heterosexuality and homosexuality, but simply says that for the irreversible homosexual there is no other way to acheive human fulfillment as a person. Thus even on the level of the moral order for this particular person, in a certain sense these actions within a loving commitment are not wrong."

Father Visser, C.SS.R. who had a share in composing the latest Decree on Sexual Ethics, leans the same way. He writes "When one is dealing with people who are so deeply homosexual that they would be in serious personal, and perhaps social trouble unless they attain a steady partnership within their homosexual lives, one can recommend to them to seek such a partnership and accept this relationship as the best they can do in the present situation." Fr. Visser bases this decision on the principle of the lesser of two evils wtih no alternative possible at the moment.

We note that Fr. Curran uses the term "irreversible" homosexuals either by birth (which is rarely verified) or by the passage of time and habit. Fr. Visser applies his principle to people "deeply homosexual." Their solutions are certainly not applicable to all.[2]

MARRIED or ORDAINED HOMOSEXUALS ?

Homosexuality presents difficulties if it be a permanent condition or even a transient urge, when the afflicted one seeks to choose a vocation in life. Since marriage is the universal inclination, the question arises whether the deviate should aspire to marriage. Today, one does read of complete conversion of homosexuals to the heterosexual state and thus marriage would be advisable. But, in general, the record is indeed poor of total stable conversion or control, sufficient to predict success in a marriage venture.

When we examine the jurisprudence of ecclesiastical courts on the subject of whether homosexual condition is a cause of nullity for a marriage we find no set norm as yet, but a trend to considering the condition as a relatively autonomous basis for nullity. The real legal image of the condition as an impediment would be "a deeply rooted character disorder, psychological inversion, homoerotic attraction and conversion with heterosexual repulsion or withdrawal." As a rule, the courts do not include the pseudo-homosexual who, in normal conditions, is a heterosexual but in times of stress or tension turns to persons of the same sex for venereal satisfaction. Once again, we must be very aware of the distinction between homosexual activity and the homosexual condition: the latter alone is the possible impediment.

It must be clear, too, that the deviate condition might be an impediment because of effects coming from the condition: such as symptomatic mental illness, psychological impotence and the exclusion of children fidelity or perpetuity from the consent. The homosexual might thus not give proper, binding marriage consent even though the condition itself, and alone, would not predicate nullity.

If we consider the condition as the possible cause of nullity we find a trend taking shape in the most recent decisions of the Roman Rota. In 1956 there was a decision unfavorable to the petitioner who maintained that her spouse had an irresistible impulse to homosexuality, because in documenting the case there was no proof of the signs of the deviate condition such as a noteworthy repugnance for heterosexual intercourse. By about 1965 there was a development in this area regarding the homosexual's ability to contract marriage. The emphasis shifted from his capacity to give real, true, marital consent namely: is the homosexual capable of binding himself and fulfilling the essential obligations of the marital relationship? Has he the capacity to assume and fulfill the rights and obligations flowing from such consent?

In 1967 a case was argued successfully in favor of the wife of a young physician who was admittedly homosexual, and who had been arrested three months after the marriage for relations with young men. The Judges discovered that the husband from the start was opposed to conjugal relations, experienced difficulties in consummating the marriage, regularly engaged from the start of the marriage in sexual relations with young men. The Court declared his marriage null on the grounds that he lacked due discretion and maturity for marriage due to his disturbed interior faculties and was not capable of due apprehension of the obligations of the married state.

Rotal jurisprudence to date has been deeply influenced by a decision by Rotal Judge Anne, Feb. 25, 1969. A lesbian married from adolescence, had ceased her homosexuality for four years after her marriage. She bore three children during this period. Then, she met up with another lesbian, practiced deviate actions, but still acted as the wife living with her husband and children. Ultimately, the husband discovered her inability to act as a true wife and mother and petitioned for an annulment of the marriage from the Roman Rota. The decision of the Rota was favorable on the grounds that since Vatican II, greater insistence must be put on the "communion of life and love" as an essential part of marital consent.

Married life is a covenant and partnership rooted in the irrevocable commitment of the parties to one another. Consent may be given but the ability to give and receive all that is contained in the consent may be found lacking.

Can one say that homosexuals are radically incapable of assuming and fulfilling marital obligations? The obligation of living the commitment to common life came under minute examination in the case and it was concluded that serious perversions of the heterosexual instinct, as is true in inverse homosexuality, preclude the establishment of the community of life which we call "marriage. This decision laid the basis for great development along juridical lines for marriage cases of many types. Did the contractants have the capacity to produce this community of life and love? Such will be the new basis for nullity.

Another interesting point the case brought out was that for a male homosexual condition a truly heterosexual community is practically impossible, whereas for the female this is not necessarily the case since a lesbian does not always find conjugal life repugnant and the condition does not quench necessarily the maternal instinct. She may lead a reasonably satisfactory conjugal life by sublimating her homosexual drives.

Should we permit the homosexual to marry? Since we deal here with a God-given natural right of marriage we must be exceedingly prudent. We quote "in reaching a decision in a particular case,

attention must be paid especially to the predomi-
nate etiology (causes of the disease), to the
chronological point of origin, to the exclusivity
of the attraction, to the motives of marriage, to
the post nuptial adjustment and to the length of
cohabitation... The ever-present question will
be: is this person, because of homosexuality, in-
curably incapable of fulfilling the basic spiritual,
affectional, emotional needs of the partner and
the children on a long term basis? If so that person is morally impotent." (Cf. Linacre Quarterly,
Aug. 1976, 204).

What about the seminarian or candidate for
the priesthood who might be a deviate? Should we
encourage him? Or, if he is a priest, what then?
It is true that God may have endowed a person
with a calling to the service of the altar and that
circumstances of environment or of nature may
have rendered this call or vocation unattainable
or undesirable for the individual. Many are at-
tracted to the religious life to fill a personal need
on a human level. And since about 4% of American males are homosexual, we must not be
abashed if we find an equal number in the clergy.

The seminarian, as well as the ordained priest,
faces all the needs common to other men if he is
to have good mental health. There is the need
of open interpersonal communication with both
sexes, the need of mental stimulation and lastly,
the need of emotional support from at least one
other significant person. It is not hard to see how
easily the person with a homosexual condition,

or one given to homosexual actions, could come into a crisis from the difficult environmental factors within which his ministry must be exercised. Homosexuality might be the main cause of the reactions but loneliness, frustration and depression — because of a personality unable to cope with the stresses and strains of the situation — are also involved. The person will be torn by conflicting desires and ideals and needs. The emotional upheaval within himself will be tremendous.

We must distinguish between the real homosexual or "condition type" and the "transient type" that is just passing through a stage. With one of the latter type, there is every chance of success through guidance and application of the procedure for eradicating a bad habit.

If the seminarian is a homosexual of condition and orientation and this has just been recently uncovered, then, it is in order to have psychiatric evaluation and strong counseling, for the homosexuality may just be the symptom of other problems.

If the seminarian or the candidate for the seminary has regularly indulged in homosexual activity in the past, and professional help gives a poor prognosis for complete chastity, happiness and peace in the religious life or in the priesthood, the doubt should be solved in favor of the Church and, the candidate should be guided into other areas of service. It might be added that the same is true of a seminarian or candidate who masturbates frequently with homosexual fantasies. This is symptomatic of deep-seated emotional problems and should be given expert attention before admittance into the religious life or the priesthood.

Counseling a homosexual priest should not point exclusively, or perhaps at all, at the reorientation of his basic sexual drives. This may not be possible in most cases. He may have to accept that orientation as his "cross" and, after having talked it out and having determined to do something about the other underlying problems of disillusionment and relationships, he should, because of his religious belief, set himself again in the total context of his community. His faith should offer him untold opportunities to grow in the love of Christ and under the inspiration of the Spirit. He can work to grow spiritually, as well as in his humanity, and begin to function as a total person with unique personal gifts for the good of the community and the Church. Unless he be a homosexual of the incurable type, he certainly can, with God's grace, hold in control the deviate urges, sublimate them and successfully carry on.

The 1969 statement of the American Catholic Bishops on Celibacy had this to say "to belong to the people, as well to fulfill our own human needs, priests must enter into many personal relationships, some of them profound. But unhealthy and self conscious preoccupations with our own personal fulfillment and rights can inhibit growth in the responsible and self-forgetting love which is the Spirit of Christ."

THE MILITANTS

So far, the theory. Now a look at two groups who have passed from theory to practice. It is one thing to be a homosexual, i.e., one whose dominant sex urge tends toward members of the same sex for erotic pleasure, and quite another to be an activist member of the Gay Liberation Movement with the avowed purpose of promoting militarily the cause of "Gay is Good" by fighting for acceptance of the homosexual condition as normal, and labelling any judgment to the contrary as discriminatory and persecutory.

The crusade has been brought to the door of the churches. The magazine, *Christian Century* called upon Protestant denominations "to get out of the business of being judgmental about our fellow human beings ... it is important to take a stand in support of the homosexual's freedom from discrimination and persecution and, on this level, nothing less than full and complete acceptance will serve." And in the Catholic Church here in the United States, Fr. John J. McNeill, S.J. has been an outspoken advocate of the same goal not only for dialogue with, but for ministry to, the homophile community.

The sore point in the controversy between the social structure, as it is now conceived, and the Gay Activist movement is the latters insistence on sexual preference as the basis of acceptance in their regard by those outside their ranks. The Churches and the social structure would prefer to accept them as human beings, as persons, worthy of respect and human kindness. It is not within our culture nor religious tenets, in general, to acknowledge the homophile condition as good and normal. It is this point that causes concern and anxiety on the part of the Christian and average citizen, no matter of what religious affiliation. The clinical and moral aspects of this condition should be given closer and impartial inquiry before any such acceptance of the condition as normal and good can possibly be countenanced. The Gay Liberation Front, the Gay Activist Alliance, refuse to agree with this approach. They decry the public attitude toward the homophile condition, an attitude which sees it as definitely evil, very undesirable, and much like a dangerous communicable disease which should be cured. They also object to the theory that it is a serious flaw in the personality of those so inclined.

Fr. Charles E. Curran in his book "*Homosexuality and Moral Theology*" marks out three Christian positions on homosexuality and its behavioral patterns. For him, homosexual actions can be wrong since they are opposed to the basic procreativity of sex; or they may be neutral; (the Quakers are supposedly thought to say that homosexuality is much like left-handedness, no better, no worse). They are, in general, wrong but for some persons this may not be true because for them, there is no other viable alternative: their condition is irreversible to that degree. For a pastoral approach to the problem, the Church must answer: are there human alternatives for the homosexual? Can the condition be partially or totally reversed? Once this question is answered, the condition will either be rejected, or given a modified acceptance both in the Church and the State.

Trends in contemporary society favor a more human liberating philosophy toward the homosexual condition. Christians believe that Christ died and rose again to liberate man from sin and death. This liberation ought to be realized in this world by man's fulfilling his nature through his own efforts seconded by God's grace and especially by experiencing God's peace. This indeed could include the homosexual, and the community's duty toward them. Such liberation must apply to the rescuing of the rich and the poor from enslavement to sin and passion, and the conversion and development of all men. This could well apply to the question at hand. As Cardinal Medeiros wrote "if we support the right of every fetus to be born, consistency demands that we equally support every man's continuing right to a truly human existence." Does this apply to the homosexual? Dare we exclude them?

Fr. George A. Kelly does not share this perspective with regard to the Gay Activist Movement. He notes the 60.000 subscribers to their newspaper the *"Advocate"* and the baneful influence of the 4000 activist "bars" across the country. He fears the number of "gay" members, supporters, promoters in high places of government and in the field of communication arts because of the harm they can do to American culture and the stability of family life. As TIME magazine concluded in its study of the movement "aside from blurring the sex roles, the most obvious aspect of the male gay culture is its promiscuity." We do not need that social problem.

Fr. Kelly accuses the gay activists of blatantly flaunting their love-life, and of not hesitating to use force to impose their ideas and achieve their goals. He points to the shameful coercing of the New York City Council in May, 1974, by a highly-agitated mob of gay-activists. He quotes police who work in "gay" neighborhoods as saying that the homophiles are prone to violence once they are organized. He cites the threat of 500 of them marching on an emergency room in a New York hospital because one of their number was fired.

Herbert Hendon, director of psycho-social services at Columbia University, bemoans the misuse of psychological data in this connection. He urges humane treatment, on an individual basis, but would never approve of imbedding these individual solutions into the society fiber for the reason that society has a high stake in the heterosexuality of its citizens. For him "gay pride" cannot be constructive for our society and to make homosexuality an alternate life-style would be disastrous.

Apart from this Movement, there is a specifically Catholic one. It is an international organization of gay and concerned Catholics called DIGNITY. Its goal is to unite gay Catholics and promote the cause of the homosexual community in a manner responsible to the church, to society and to the individual homosexual. It held its first national convention in September 1973.

As of May 1976, *Dignity* had 46 chapters in 22 States, in the District of Columbia, in Puerto Rico and in Canada. It is affiliated with many international organizations of the same nature such as "Acceptance" in Australia, "Quest" in England, "Veritas" in Sweden. The membership is estimated at 5,000. It chooses to work within the Catholic Church but has no official standing; it aims to influence the Church in her position and teaching on the matter of homosexuality. It has a monthly publication which bears the name DIGNITY, now in its seventh volume.

Dignity feels a change slowly coming in the Catholic Church. It has declared "More and more, the Gay Catholic is able to see the image of Christ in his priest. He knows more and more priests in whom he sees a Good Shepherd, one who serves, one who hungers and thirsts for social justice, one who doesn't hesitate to eat and drink with those whom society shuns, a father who loves his children."

Dignity seeks acceptance and full participation in the life of the Church, as homosexuals, for those who are in this condition. It leans to the theory "that homosexuality constitutionally irreversible, represents a natural variation of mammalian sexual behavior and is intrinsically good when it is expressed in an ethically responsible, unselfish and Christian manner, as all sexuality must be. In their charter of beliefs we read that "Gay Catholics are members of Christ's mystical body and numbered among the people of God . . . we have an inherent dignity because God created us, Christ died for us, the Holy Spirit sanctified us in Baptism, making us His temple . . . because of all this, we have the right, the privilege, the duty, to live the sacramental life . . . we believe that Gays can express their sexuality in a manner that is consonant with Christ's teachings . . ."

This view, while sincere, is not the view of the *Declaration on Sexual Ethics.* Whilst sympathetic to those afflicted with the homosexual condition, this document states plainly "homosexual acts are intrinsically disordered and can in no case be approved of." It does admit that, apparently, there are people who are homosexuals as a result of some kind of innate instinct as well as those who have "acquired" this condition, and it recognizes how difficult it will be for all homosexuals to change, especially the former type. The Church holds out hope and a helping hand to all of them. It encourages all to make the effort to cooperate with God's grace, and to expect eventual victory.

Cf. Linacre Quarterly, August, 1976: *Hate The Sin, but Love the Sinner. Sin? What sin?* by John F. Russell, J.D., pp. 179-192.

Cf. Homiletic and Pastoral Review: March, 1976, p. 10: *A Second Look at the Gay Activist Movement* by Geo. A. Kelly.

Cf. Theological Studies: *Notes on Moral Theology*, March, 1972, 112-119.

PART 2

ABORTION

The high incidence of abortions in our country stirs the emotions of men and women of all creeds and political affiliations. In New York City alone, for the year 1975, the number of abortions rose to about 100,000. It said that, on the average, there is an abortion every two or three minutes per day. The sex revolution of the last decade or so brought to the fore a philosophy that has little sensitivity for the unborn child.

Strangely enough on a very vital issue such as this, some people take a situational ethic approach: if abortion is useful to them at the moment, it will be their choice; how they feel on the question at the time they are contemplating it, rules their decision. Other considerations, such as the Law of God, reverence for the gift of human life seem to matter very little. The contemporary world has been weaned away from moral rectitude on this subject. The campaign again the rights of the unborn has been expertly waged through every medium of communication. During the years 1967-1970, the classified library reference file listed under the topic "abortion" over 1400 authors!

ETHIC EROSION

Years ago, medical men debated whether the product of human conception in all stages of development in the womb, was truly human. Today, the dictum: "whatever is born of woman is human" is well accepted by the general consensus. The modern rejoinder is: "so what"? As one medical author remarked "I ADMIT THAT IT IS HUMAN BUT I feel that the mother's wishes are more important than the child's." An editorial in the California Journal of Medicine sets the tone. Under the title "A New Ethic for Medicine and Society" we read "the traditional Western ethic has always placed great emphasis on the intrinsic worth and equal value of every human life ... an ethic common to the Judaeo-Christian heritage ... but an erosion of this ethic is taking place and since the old ethic has not been fully displaced, it has been necessary to separate from the concept of abortion, the idea of killing which continues to be socially abhorrent. The result has been a curious avoidance of the scientific fact which everyone knows, that human life begins at conception and continues, whether it be intra or extra uterine, until death." The author goes on to say that all life is sacred; consequently, all doctors should begin to recognize it for what it is, prepare to apply it in a rational way for the fulfillment and betterment of mankind in a world that soon will be a biologically-oriented world society." [1]

A VALUE SYSTEM

We fail, sometimes, to realize how much our own value system colors our convictions and the answers to serious problems. In a pluralistic society such as ours, we have to understand clearly our position on an issue and to try to understand that of our neighbor, even if we cannot always accept his answer to the problem. The Catholic sees abortion as the murder of an innocent human being: his religious convictions permit no other conclusion. The liberal scientist will see the issue only as one related to bringing down a disastrously high birth rate. The radical feminist will bewail the poverty of so many married women in dire need of relief through abortion with only the services of the unskilled at her command. Her remedy for such conditions will be to legitimize abortion on demand. The fundamentalist will oppose legal abortion because it opens the door to further abuse of the sex faculty by reason of sexual degradation, of heinous crimes of infanticide, and of child abuse.

On the issue of abortion, a great division of opinion is generated by differing approaches: some contend that human life and personhood appear from the first moment of fertilization; others staunchly defend the thesis that human *life* is present but that we should be more pre-occupied with human *personhood* and until that is achieved, the fetus is expendable (and the widest latitude of time is given to the moment of personhood's appearance). Other views and approaches will be found in the following pages.

WHAT IT IS

Direct abortion for the Catholic is the dislodging and expelling of a living fetus from the mother's womb before it is able to live, outside the womb, on its own or by means of a mechanical device. The object of *direct* abortion is to rid the womb of a fetus not yet viable outside the womb. It is *indirect* abortion if the object of the procedure is not the fetus. If the fetus is accidentally expelled as a secondary effect of the procedure, as in the case of an operation for a diseased appendix on a pregnant woman, it is indirect abortion. The agent's action is directed at the disease, not the fetus.

The fetus is deemed viable 28 weeks after conception. With skilled care and the use of the incubator it may possibly be viable 20 to 24 weeks after conception. To take a child from its mother's womb before the minimum of 20 to 28 weeks is abortion. After that time, but before the full nine months, it is premature birth.

THE PROCESS OF FETAL DEVELOPMENT

The fetus is presumed *alive* from the first
moment of conception. Whether it is a *human
being* at that moment is open to discussion. But,
by whatever name we know it, the zygote (cell
formed by the union of 2 others) is human since
it is born of woman, conceived in woman. The
physical process of fetal development helps us
to understand and evaluate the dissent on this
topic of abortion.

The sperm fertilizes the ovum in the oviduct
and not in the womb. This fertilization is not really a moment, but a process which may take up
to four hours or more before the full chromosomal
conjunction and full fertilization occurs. Experts
write 'fertilization is complete with the metaphase
of the first cleavage to a two cell stage." This is
an ovicellular phenomenon and the entire process
can stop at this stage without the mother organism
becoming pregnant or fertile. The majority of
sperm ovum conjunctions do not eventuate as
babies. Witsche estimates that 58% never reach
implantation; that 16% cease at the time of conjunction and only 30% survive until birth.

DNA

Human life is transmitted in the living DNA
(desoxyribonucleic acid) of the cell. It is this
which is alive and splits itself into copies of itself
and transmits its physicochemical energy. The
sperm-ovum-zygote, the free skin-graft, tissue-
culture cell, all are biologically-living from this

energy. The zygote lives but its "livingness" ante-dates the existence of the zygote.

RNA

The splitting of the zygote into copies of itself is not yet proof of its hominality since it can happen artificially, and it is attested by scientists that even the phenomenon of cleavage (cell division) can occur in an unfertilized ovum. This cleavage happens within 40 to 50 hours after fertilization and continues at such a rapid pace that the cell count can run up in the millions without any increase in weight or volume of the cell mass. Between the 4th to the 8th stage of cleavage, the cell mass descends into the uterine cavity and begins the nidation site, boring into the uterine lining. This activity has been directed by the RNA (ribonucleic acid) from the mother's ovum. The zygote has remained independent, from a nutritional aspect, of the mother. True, there has been a process of osmosis of a salt but no elemental sugars or proteins can be utilized until implanation has been completed. After 14 to 22 days of activity under the RNA, the internal activity of the zygote will be under the direction of a RNA factor elaborated by the conceptus itself.

DIFFERENTIATIONS

At this point, the cell mass is capable of differentiating into any type of subsequent cell such as the blood, bone or brain. The first of these differentiations is that of the placenta and the same cells give out as early as one week after fertilization, a hormone called "Human Chorion Gonadatrophin." Even the presence of this hormone does not assure us that it is a human fetus, a pregnancy, if we are to believe the experts. The cell mass continues to grow, and the second differentiation is that of the primordial brain tissue; the 14th day sees the appearance of the heart tissue, This, too, is the moment of twinning. The fetus may split into two halves and, if each succeeds in growing, two adults will appear. The two halves may again join and only one adult will be born, or the halves may remain joined only in one area and we will have Siamese twins.

THE HOMINAL ORGANIZER

The cell at fertilization comprises 46 chromosomes (47 for a Mongoloid). It is of human order but as yet no hominality is claimed for it. The zygote's phenotype i.e. the sum of apparitional characteristics of the child's physical make-up which have been derived from hereditary sources and handed down in each newly generated link, is firmly established at fertilization. The individuality of the zygote is constituted in the biological order — its unity, uniqueness, induplicability. At the end of the second week, or at the beginning of the third, a very important factor appears: it is the "hominal organizer" and it appears on the lower pole of the blastula (early embryo). It is formed by a thin layer of fluid between the placenta and the inner cell mass. Without this primary organizer no further differentiation could take place. Once in place, the specific organs of "homo," man appear.

It is at this stage that the hominizable products of fertilization and the non-hominizable products are distinguished. The irrevocable unity of the individual is established, twinning can no longer take place and reconjunction cannot occur. Many scientists favor this moment for ensoulment and of hominization. A Catholic doctor writes "I submit that we can justifiably hold that at fertilization is laid down only the characteristics of the subsequently hominizable entity; hominization and individualization of which cannot be posited until the late second or early third week after fertilization." (Dr. Diamond, Theol. Studies, June 1975).

SELF-NOURISHING

From the very start the free zygote and its developments have lived off themselves in a sort of self-consuming modality. Eventually these cells must find a fully functional source of nutrition, else they will die. The self-sustaining blastula evolves around the 14th day after fertilization, or some 7 to 10 days afterwards, depending on special circumstances. Once the child's circulatory and cardiac system functions, a source of nutrition on its own is a "must." The heart beat is heard at the end of the third week or around the 23rd day. It is then that the embryo enters the maternal circulatory system and its very life depends on its ability to utilize extrinsics.

This is another reason why biologists, in view of these vital events converging in that period of the 14th to the 23rd day after fertilization, are inclined to see hominization and personhood, taking place two or three weeks after fertilization. To them, there is no compelling reason to see it taking place before that period. The geneticist following this theory of hominization will not see abortion verified until the fetus is 3 weeks old. Prior to that time, expelling the fetus will not be considered "homicide" because of the doubt as to the presence of ensoulment, of hominization. To verify abortion in the strict sense for the geneticist there must be a development of the entity in the womb and the fetus must be capable of carrying out the minimal acts of continued existence on its own. At fertilization this is certainly not present genetically; the most one can say is that "homo" is potentially present.[1]

THE JUDEO-CHRISTIAN VIEWPOINT

Holy Writ makes no philosophical observations as to the moment when human life begins in the womb; but it does mention in many places, that the period which precedes birth is the object of God's special providence. God creates, forms, molds the human being in His hand. Cf. Ps. 118, Ps. 22, 71, 139; John IV, v. 5; Luke I, v. 44; Is. 49, vv. 1-5; Job 10, v. 8. Exodus has an interpolated proviso with a penalty for abortion accidentally brought about, and one for miscarriage. (Ex. 21, v. 22). The passages relative to the birth of John the Baptist, the circumstances surrounding the birth of Christ (Mary's pregnancy prior to her marriage to Joseph) indicate the belief in the reality of life in the womb as human life in its fullness.

TRADITION

The more explicit source of Christian condemnation of abortion is found in Tradition. The
Book of Didache, (c. 80 A.D.) ranks it as a grievous sin, forbidden by the Decalogue. The Epistle
of Barnabas (c. 138 A.D.) says "you shall not
slay the child by abortion." And Tertullian wrote
"It is not lawful to destroy what is conceived in
the womb while the blood is still being formed
into man."

During the fifth century more attention was
paid to the moment of ensoulment and the distinction of "formed and unformed fetus" was in-
troduced. It was murder to abort a formed fetus;
it was a serious sin to do so to an unformed. John
Noonan writes "By 450 the teaching on abortion
both for the East as well as for the West was set
out with clarity and substantial consistency. There
was a distinction accepted by some as to the
unformed embryo, some consequent variations in
the analysis of sin in this regard, some local differences as to penances necessary to expiate such
a sin. The cultures of secular societies had accepted
abortion but the Christians, men of both the
Greco and Roman empire and of the Gospel, condemned it. The Christian rule was certain." (Noonan: Abortion and the Catholic Church, p. 19).

St. Jerome and St. Augustine used the terms
"formed" and "unformed"; never was there any
relenting on the grave nature of the sin of abortion
of the formed or unformed fetus. Gratian in his
Decrees wrote "he is a murderer who brings
about abortion before the soul is in the body."

The Decretals of Gregory did the same, but Pope Sixtus in 1588 refused the distinction of formed and unformed, contradicted eminent theologians such as Liguori and Lessius, and decreed that every abortion was homicide. Pius IX agreed with his predecessor and penalized every abortion with excommunication.

THE CHURCH TODAY

The 1918 Code of Canon Law in c. 2350 punishes all those procuring abortion with excommunication; c. 985 makes it the basis of an irregularity for clerics; c. 747 commands that every fetus, no matter when aborted, be baptized at least under condition and c. 746 permits baptism in the womb, if necessary. By this baptism, the human being, no matter how old, becomes a child of God and also a person in the Church.

Pope John XXIII in *Mater et Magistra* wrote "Human life is sacred; from its very inception, the creative action of God is directly operative." Vatican II in "Church in the Modern World" declared "from the first moment of its conception, life must be guarded with the greatest care while abortion and infanticide are unspeakable crimes."

Pope Paul VI in *Humanae Vitae* says "in conformity with these landmarks in the human and Christian vision of marriage, we must declare again that the direct interruption of the generative process already begun, and above all, directly willed and procured abortion, even for therapeutic reasons, are absolutely to be excluded

as licit means of regulating birth." The Church
has never wavered in its teaching that abortion,
directly willed, is a serious offense.

Fr. John Magnan, S.J. could write "the teaching on abortion is based sufficiently on solid
foundation for the Church to maintain, in practice, that all direct abortions, as a means to an
end, or as an end in themselves, are contrary to
divine law and this admits of no exception." [1]

This Church position favors immediate ensoulment from the moment of fertilization. Full
humanity, the person itself, would be conferred
at that moment. But the respect to life due the
fetus and the unrelenting opposition of the Church
to abortion do not rest on that theory alone. The
Church proclaims that human life is there from
the beginning, even if personhood is not actually
present, and is present as a sacred gift of God
which is preparing for, calling for a soul, (personhood). It merits and demands our reverence.

Footnote no. 19 of the Vatican Declaration on
Abortion of June 28, 1974 (Origins, Dec. 12, 1974,
p. 392), says: "The Declaration expressly leaves
aside the question of the moment when the spiritual soul is infused. There is not unanimous tradition on this point, and authors are in disagreement. For some, it dates from the first instant,
whilst for others it could not precede nidation
(at least nidation). It is not within the competence of science to decide between these views,
because the existence of an immortal soul is not
a question in its field. It is a philosophical problem from which our moral affirmation remains in-

dependent for two reasons: first, even supposing belated animation, there is still present nothing less than human life, preparing for, calling for a soul in which the nature received from the parents is completed. Secondly, it suffices that this presence of the soul be probable, (and one cannot prove the contrary) in order that the taking of life involve accepting the risk of killing a man, not only waiting for, but already in possession of his soul."

In paragraph 12 we read "Respect for human life is called for from the time that the process of generation begins. From the time the ovum is fertilized, a life is begun which is neither that of the father, nor of the mother; it is rather the life of a new human being with his own growth. It would be made human, if it were not already human." And again, "from a moral viewpoint this is certain; even if a doubt existed concerning whether the fruit of conception is already a human person, it is objectively a grave sin to risk murder — the one who *will be* a man, is *already* one" (par. no. 13).

SALIENT POINTS OF THE DECLARATION

1. The Church is vowed to defend the dignity of man.

2. The Church views human life as a sacred in His sight; man will be held accountable for its gift from God; it bears His image; it is precious when his stewardship is over.

3. Human life must be favored from the very first moment of fertilization and at all stages of development.

4. Despite differences of opinion as to the precise moment of ensoulment, it has always been taught that procured abortion from the first days of fertilization, is objectively a grave sin.

5. Man's right to life is basic to man; it comes from God and is antecedent to any recognition by society, or any legitimate authority. MAN MAY SACRIFICE IT FOR A HIGHER VALUE or risk it for the same value, but he himself must never be treated as a means to an end.

6. This respect for human life must prevail from the first moment of fertilization since, from then on, a new human life has begun with its own growth, quite distinct from its parents.

7. It is a serious sin to risk murder in attacking the zygote's life even if one is in doubt as to the presence of the human soul at that moment.

8. Regardless of different opinions as to the exact moment of ensoulment, and their theoretical value, the Church embraces the thesis that from the first moment of fertilization, there is nothing less than a human life in the womb, preparing for and calling for a soul by which the nature, received from parents, will be completed. Reverence is due to this life and, since the presence of the soul is probable (no proof to the contrary is possible), in any attempted abortion there is always the risk of killing a human person.[2]

CONTEMPORARY NON-CATHOLIC THOUGHT

Professor Williams of the Harvard Divinity School claims that vast sectors of liberal Protestant and Jewish opinion support the strict doctrine of Catholic views on abortion. "In contemporary American culture both the National Council of Churches and Evangelical Protestantism (along with the General Assembly of the 60,000-member Presbyterian Church in America) have expressed opposition to abortion."

But, Protestants are much less bound to Tradition than to the Bible, and thus have been more influenced by culture and science. The professor asserts that the more Christians insist on procreation as the primary end of marriage, the greater the opposition to abortion. The more they view mutual trust and companionship as primary, the less opposition. He cites the fact that the Puritans were of the latter class and that this tradition has been handed down even to our contemporaries in the Protestant churches.[3]

PRO-LIFE MOVEMENT

In 1976 the Catholic Church in the United States, along with many other persons of different religious denominations, waged a campaign under the slogan "Right to Life" with the ultimate goal of obtaining an amendment to the U.S. Constitution forbidding abortion on demand. The chief objection against this action by the Church was that it violated the American concept of religious freedom. It was argued that a constitutional amendment AND THE CONSEQUENT passage of restrictive abortion laws would violate, infringe upon, or constrain religious freedom as protected under the First Amendment. If passed, such an amendment would incorporate the teachings of one church and thus lead to the establishment of an official religion.

Archbishop Bernardin before the Senate Judiciary Committee commented: "There is a religious non-issue on the subject of abortion and this is embodied in the assertion that efforts by religious persons on behalf of a constitutional amendment to protect human life are somehow inappropriate. Abortion is not wrong simply because the Catholic Church or any church says that it is wrong. Abortion is wrong, in and of itself.

"It is true that the Catholic Church, and many other churches teach that abortion is wrong just as they teach that racial discrimination is wrong, that exploitation of the poor is wrong, that all injustice, and injury to others are wrong. So in my case, and that of many other religious persons, religious doctrine powerfully reinforces our commitment to human rights. We are publicly committed on a broad range of domestic and international issues. Within the past week alone, the Bishops, continuing a practice of many years' standing have testified before committees of Congress on full employment and on food stamps. No objections are raised when we give voice to our moral convictions on such matters as these, and that is the way it should be. For it is not religious doctrine that we wish to see enacted into law;

it is respect for human dignity and human rights; and specifically in this case, the right to life itself. Our country faces a startling and terrifying fact. With the approval of the law, indeed with the sanction of the highest court, one million human lives are destroyed each year by abortion in these United States. Considerations of health, or economic distress cannot account for this appalling situation. The plain fact is that many, if not all, of these million lives are destroyed because others find it convenient to destroy them. By the hundreds of thousands each year we are killing the unborn for convenience's sake" (Origins, Apr. 8, '76, 664).

In concluding their appeal to the Committee on Judicial Matters, the Bishops declared "we reject any assertion or implication that the Catholic Church, in exercising its rights to uphold and speak out in favor of the fundamental right to life, is in fact, attempting to impose its morality on the nation. We further reject the assertion that unless a constitutional amendment, or a restrictive abortion law proceeds from a wholly secular purpose, it must be rejected as an attack on the First amendment. Moreover, we oppose initiatives of the State to endorse and promote abortion on request in social policies and health care programs as an inappropriate exercise of State power, and as a violation of the religious liberty of those who do not wish to support, or pay for permissive abortion. Finally, we believe that the right to amend the Constitution is in fact, a right protected by the First and Ninth Amendments ... and we would be remiss in our duty if we were to refrain from speaking in behalf of human life and ensuring the development of a system of justice that provides legal protection for the right to life of all human beings born and unborn." (Cf. Origins, April, 1976, p. 667).

The Church position on the abortion issue is inspired by convictions concerning human dignity, the right to life of the unborn, the responsibility of the state to protect basic human rights. It is, by no means, inspired by a desire to impose its morality on the overall society. Human dignity is an inherent value of the human person and this concept has been enshrined in law from time immemorial.

THE REAL ISSUE

The real opposition to the Catholic position revolves around its insistence that protection be given the fetus from the earliest stage of fertilization. It contends that all scientific data indicate that once the sperm and the ovum have united there is the beginning of (at least) a potential human being; that the zygote will develop and has everything for that process within itself. If it meets with no interference, it will grow into actual birth and begin the phase of infancy. Whether it is a human *person*, in the philosophical sense or not, matters little, because it is human *life*. Catholics contend that we should respect it, reverence it, protect it from the moment of fertilization. It is, very probably, a human person from that same moment, so in case of doubt, we must favor the fetus.

THE MEDICAL VIEWPOINT

It is pretty much conceded today that human life is present in the embryo since biological studies can establish that life generated by humans begins to differ significantly from any other life from the earliest moments; but no precise moment can be singled out as its actual beginning.

There is substantial agreement, among scientists, that the *presence* of human life in the earliest stages is not the same as saying that the *fulness* of human life, personhood, is present at that moment. Church opinion makes the conferral of personhood coincide with the ensoulment of the fetus. Others watch for specific human development postulating personal attributes.

DR. DIAMOND'S CONTENTION

This Catholic surgeon of eminent reputation feels that personhood is not conferred at the moment of fertilization. His basic challenge is: the biological data about the early zygote's activity render simply implausible any philosophical concept of human i.e., personal, life which allows the killing of early unborn human life to be considered homicidal. (He does not admit personhood at that moment — homicide is killing a human person). He contends that the individual zygote is irrevocably established ONLY when the primary organizer appears, since before that moment, twinning and reconjunction of a twinned morula (solid mass of cells produced during early development), or a split morula can possibly occur. Cells cannot become differentiated into different organs unless the primary organizer appears. This will happen late in the second or early in the third week after fertilization so that hominization and individuation of the zygote cannot be established until that moment. It is then, and only then, that we might speak of "homicide" if the fetus were to be destroyed. (Cf. Linacre Quarterly, May, 1976, p. 90).

A PRO-LIFE PROBLEM

This medical view seems to strike a serious blow at Pro-Life views. Not exactly. The basic act by which the fertilized ovum becomes a human being requires a definite amount of initial cell matter if specific organs are to develop in the zygote. Once this amount is present, development can begin. Part of such development will be the appearance of the "primary organizer." The appearance of this factor is rooted in the fundamental tendency of the zygote, because it is required to ensure that the vegetative structure of the primitive cell develop.

For this reason, it can be said that the primary organizer is *already contained* in the zygote and has simply been awaiting the right moment to become operative. *It is not something super-added.* And so the fertilized ovum should be protected in virtue of its dignity as a principle in human generation. (Linacre Quarterly, May, 1976, p. 113).

TWINNING

Does twinning preclude the existence of ONE person from the moment of fertilization? No. Identical twins exist and one of them must be related to the initial conjunction of ovum and sperm. Does it then split in two? There is no peremptory argument proving that the basic tendential principle in both twins began in the SAME fertilized ovum. One could have begun at fertilization, and the other at the moment of twinning. It can simply be presumed that the principle of human life exists in each process of fertilization, and is present when a human soul is infused, whether this be at the moment of conception, of fertilization at the conjunction of the sperm and the ovum, or at the "morula" stage of development as in the case of twins.

Twinning is not as critical a piece of evidence against the presence of personhood at fertilization as it is claimed to be. (Cf. Linacre Quarterly, 1976, p. 91).

DR. DUPRE'S COMPROMISE

Professor Dupre of Yale's Department of Religious Studies writes at length of the distinction between humanity and personhood. That human life is present in the embryo is well established by the biological sciences though, for the Doctor, no one moment can be singled out as to its inception. The most undisputable moment would be that of the attaching of the specifically-human frontal part of the cortex to the rest of the brain. This occurs in the third month after birth so it cannot be held as the inception of human life. The exact moment of the achievement of personhood by the embryo we do not know. Besides, it will depend on the issues discussed just when minimum conditions are required for this; and certain functions will always be presumed.

Dr. Dupre alleges that personhood is underived and unless we wish to engender confusion it must be assumed that the moment of the appearance of personhood coincides with that of the beginning of human life-minimally at least. But personhood is a dynamic entity which reaches its peak gradually and sometimes never gets that far even in maturity. It introduces an element not contained in the human embryo as such. It is an active process, a self-determining structure which unfolds gradually and the degree of actuality enters into the very essence of personhood (at any given moment). By it the human being gradually becomes self-determined and this process embraces the newborn infant to a degree.

Dupre is convinced that human life is attacked from the very first moment of fertilization when abortion is considered; and if this is so, then an inchoate personhood is also the object of the attack. But since personhood is a gradual achievement by the fetus, each person's right to life is not the same but varies according to its stage of development. What would be sanctioned in the beginning stages of pregnancy would not be sanctioned in the later period.

In times of open conflict between the mother's life and the continuation of pregnancy, in cases of rape, or in the avoidance of major, communal injustice the solution might hinge on the seriousness of the threat to life and the stage of development of human life of the fetus. He asks: what is the right course when severe retardation (mentally) is detected before actual birth? Would severely diminished personhood justify abortion particularly at an advanced stage of pregnancy? He answers "I do not know, but whatever it may be, it certainly cannot be reached on the basis of simplistic principles such as "the woman alone has a right over her body," or "a personal life should never be extinguished." The eminent professor says the real difficulty in applying developmental views as to personhood is that there is no easy rule of thumb for moral decisions. It is an objective method that must be applied on a sliding scale.[1]

PSYCHOLOGICAL CONFLICT

Some see abortion as a necessary remedy when the mother suffers devastating effects from the fact that she is pregnant. Studies along this line of thought are sparse but we can appreciate that pregnancy is a major event in the life of any woman and possibly could be a crisis. Bearing a child will influence the woman's attitude toward herself, her body, her husband and her children. Stress is bound to come from the uncertainty of the outcome (especially after a certain age) and of the financial burden it imposes. It can be the source of heavy emotional, mental and physical reactions.

Psychologically, the woman may go through several neurotic phases: especially one of rejection of self because of her ambivalence toward child-bearing, toward rearing of children, and toward her uncertain, feminine role. She may have severe fears of not being able to give birth to healthy progeny, or fears of the deterioration of her own body as a result of pregnancy, or the added burden of a child may bother her. She may vacillate between the deepest depression and the state of elation. If this is true of the married woman, how much more so of the unmarried who becomes pregnant! To measure this stress and strain is difficult because the sum total of such responses will depend greatly on the social psychological and cultural content of the woman's own childhood, of her background and of the projected future of her married life. But we can conclude that pregnancy is a period of abnormal stress and could become a life-devastating stage.

NEUROSES-PSYCHOSES

Psychiatric indications could thus arise for the pregnant woman. For the past ten years the trend has been upward for abortions on this score. Psychiatrists differ as to the causative agent of psychosis which appears in pregnant or new-mothers. Most claim that a certain amount of psychosis preexisted the pregnancy but that the pregnancy incited the latent illness or exacerbated it. There is a study of 103 cases of psychotic reactions associated with pregnancy which indicate, as a universal reaction, the rejection of the new born either in fact, or symbolically, by actual attempts at infanticide. The current wave of "battered children" may be a delayed reaction to the psychological hostility toward the "unwanted child." Other studies tend to show that children born of psychotic parents do suffer mentally from their close association with the parents; and we must remember there is no deprivation greater for a child than this sort of rejection.

DISTURBED MOTHERS

Some data gathered in a survey of 30 women in St. Louis, who had mental illness prior to their pregnancies, indicate that there was, on the part of the women, a rejection of the female, biological role and the presence of sadomasochistic impulses. They sought abortions after a voluntary pregnancy to fulfill conflicting desires within themselves: the pregnancy fulfilled the unconscious masochistic wish, while the abortion satisfied both the sadistic and masochistic desires.

Another psychologist contends that the attitudes of the pregnant woman will affect the fetus and that emotional strain during pregnancy could well contribute to difficult deliveries and defective progeny. But we must conclude, with Daniel Callahan that "there is still much that is not known about the relationship between a woman and her fetus and not much more is known about the relationship of the mother to her new-born child. Both areas are open to considerable controversy... That there is some relationship of importance in both cases is reasonable to presume... but just what that relationship is, (apart from the most extreme circumstances) is much less clear than one would wish."

PSYCHIATRIC INDICATIONS

What criteria would indicate the need of psychiatric intervention in the case of a pregnant woman, and possibly the need of abortion because of such illness? There is a considerable diversity of opinion on this score.

All admit, that with intensive care, any woman can be brought through a pregnancy in no worse shape than when she entered it. But we cannot deny that pregnancy and childbirth can precipitate and aggravate psychological illness. An abnormal psychological condition prior to the pregnancy coupled with the anxiety of pregnancy, plus social stress that cannot be relieved by ordinary therapeutic measures, could easily cause a grave, psychiatric condition. Basic to this illness would be deep depression, suicidal tendencies, mental retardation, poor family relationships and hostility. The toll of all these factors cannot be truly evaluated except in terms of the woman's entire life and background. It cannot be treated as a separate entity. The medical decision would need in its formation much mature judgment and prudence.

We could not sanction abortion according to the common doctrine of the Church but we would counsel the anxious woman and give her every advantage, morally and medically available.[2]

EVERY WOMAN?

Is pregnancy a traumatic experience for every woman? There is an opinion that anyone who seeks an abortion is already a disturbed personality. Authoress May E. Roman writes "the very fact that a woman cannot tolerate pregnancy, or is in intense conflict, is an indication that the pre-pregnant personality of this woman was immature and, in this sense, can be labeled as psycho-pathological; ... in some cases it is an unresolved oedipal situation, and in others, exaggerated narcissism; the latter could well be present in all cases." Will the abortion cause a trauma? It could well be a potential major trauma to a woman because of its emotional significance. How can a woman who is conditioned to look upon abortion as evil, be conditioned to feel that abortion is morally good? All psychiatrists stress an ambivalence in women about abortion: they are divided in themselves; in their hearts, they may well want to have the baby whose birth they are about to prevent; they feel uneasy about the situation deep down; for after all it is an event that had a beginning, and now the progress of that event is about to be stopped — it is no mere contraceptive technique. The statistics present a very mixed picture. The most common denominator of them would be that 25% of those who undergo abortions will show observable, psychological sequelae, either mild or severe, and it would be a guilt reaction. Much will depend upon the women's general stance toward abortion and the contexts of their pregnancy from a cultural, personal, familial, social standpoint. So each woman would have to be judged on a personal basis as to her particular background, situation, sensitivity to values concerning abortions etc. Psychiatric material on the whole does not tell us much more on this point.[3]

A CASE

We end this topic wtih the following case submitted by a doctor from actual practice in order to induce readers to appreciate the serious problems that this area of psychological and psychiatric illnesses can bring to light. What to do in this case? Often this woman is depressed, although not suicidal, she is assured of the possibility of an abortion. If the husband and doctor refuse this possibility then the risk for suicide increases even to the point of requiring long hospitalization for 6 to 9 months through pregnancy. This may mean admission to a State hospital since the family cannot afford a private mental hospital. The doctor is reluctant to send the patient to the undesirable, State hospital. What should he do? You can well be sure that the spectre of abortion hangs realistically over the doctor's head. There is a feeling of frustration and inadequacy in psychiatric circles when confronted with serious problems, for so little research is being done, and so little money appropriated, for progress in this branch of medico-psychological-psychiatric practice.[4]

THE MORAL VIEWPOINT

Nowhere more than among medical and nursing staffs does the issue of abortion generate more stress and anxiety. In particular, any attempt to use a Catholic health facility for procedures contrary to Church norms often imposes an intolerable burden on staff and administration.

The Catholic hospital is not just a function of charity and mercy but must be concerned with the rights of the patient for it is considered a community health resource; it serves a pluralistic community; it is often partially subsidized by government funds; and the community, itself, aids the hospital financially for maintenance and expansion. It is no longer an enterprise of a religious community but one in which other voices must be heard as to policy etc. Then, too, in our day freedom of conscience is much more stressed and we are more inclined to respect the moral convictions of others even though we do disagree with them. Such circumstances make it rather difficult to enforce moral principles and policies built on them; occasionally, to do so is very undesirable. While we cannot advocate the by-passing of these moral imperatives, we must admit that extreme prudence and understanding are called for today in hospital public policy.

Archbishop James Hayes of Canada some years back foresaw this condition when he said "it is the character of the role (of the Catholic hospital) that is in question. Public authority will continue to assume more administrative and policy-making responsibility. The bearing of Christian witness in the promotion of Christian ethical standards will be the responsibility of the staff and the practitioner... moral judgment and responsibility will be taken out of the hands of the Catholic administration, and will reside in the individual Catholic or Christian conscience. The Code of medical ethics must speak to the conscience of Catholic doctors and nurses but we must allow the maximum possible scope for action in their professional work. The hospital must show an unwavering confidence in their willingness and ability to assume moral responsibility for their actions" (Address to the Cath. Hosp. Association in 1968).

Fr. Richard McCormick agrees that the Catholic hospital will, in the future, find itself in a position of tolerating practices which by its own directives, are totally inappropriate and in which

the administrators will be playing a subsidiary
role in medico-moral decisions. It will happen
that the doctor or patient will be found doing
something immoral as per the Catholic norm and
the Administration will be obliged to bring the
matter to expert attention but with an overall
mentality of toleration and cooperation; it will
be in this spirit that witness to Christ's love will
be most effective rather than by causing undue
harm through strict enforcement of an ideal Catholic solution. Fr. McCormick says "I am not arguing
for the Catholic hospital to abandon moral policies. I am arguing that all must tolerate certain
deviations from the approved Code." He does feel
that the problem of tolerance must be adequately
faced and harmonized with fidelity to the basic
mission of the Catholic hospital. (Chicago Studies,
1972, 312).[1]

ACUTE CASES

In a society fond of bringing malpractice suits,
we can appreciate the wisdom of the above quo-
tation. What if a doctor is in group practice, and
it is his night to carry the load, and an operation
is scheduled that he deems is immoral — what shall
he, or can he do? — once everything is ready and
no delay can be tolerated? If a patient is sent on
an emergency call from another hospital and in
the process of complying with the directives, it
is found that they involve a licit operation with
a secondary procedure of an illicit nature, and
there is no time to waste for an adjustment; if
the patient is transferred to another facility, there

is the risk of death; if the patient will not let the operation proceed unless both procedures are to be included — what is to be done? We cannot deny the anxiety on the part of any Catholic doctor in such trying cases. Fr. McCormick was perhaps thinking in such terms. As Fr. Drinan, S.J. has remarked 'there are no easy solutions or ready options for the Catholic doctor, legislator or jurist on the question of abortion and the law."

IN THE HOSPITAL

In the Catholic hospital obviously the basic rules applies: any deliberate attempt directly to deprive a fetus or embryo of its life is immoral. No such hospital may provide abortion services nor make its facilities or personnel available for this purpose.

It is a serious sin for hospital personnel to perform or obtain abortions or to persuade others to do so. Primarily responsible is the doctor in the case but all who willingly and deliberately assist in abortion procedures share the sinfulness: e.g., those who administer abortifacient drugs. Responsibility would not ordinarily extend to those who merely prepare patients for the procedure or provide after-care — unless this would be interpreted to mean that they, too, consider that the unborn child has no right to life.

Every procedure whose sole immediate attempt is the termination of pregnancy before viability is an abortion (and this includes procedures affecting the interval between conception and implantation of the embryo).

Operations, treatments and medications which do not directly intend termination of pregnancy but which have as their purpose the cure of a proportionately serious pathological condition of the mother are permitted even though the fetus may be indirectly killed. If it is not certainly dead, it should be baptized.

Hysterectomy even during pregnancy and before viability of the fetus is permitted as is the removal of any pathological condition if the operation cannot be postponed.

THE NURSE AND ABORTION

The nurse cannot approve of an immoral act; she may never knowingly and willingly assist at an abortion. May she cooperate in any manner? She may give remote material cooperation to avoid the loss of her position, great inconvenience, loss of personal gain. She cooperates but does not approve and she lets it be known. The closer and more necessary the cooperation in an unethical act, then the more pressing the reason required for material cooperation.

She must never cooperate in such a manner that an observer would reasonably draw the conclusion that she was agreeing with the act. She must never perform, even partially, the act such as abortion. She may do in illicit acts what, by profession, she would do in a licit procedure: for example, hand the instruments or sterilize them. A sufficient reason would always justify mediate material cooperation. If her refusal would bring grave loss to self, or to another loss of life, reputation, or serious personal harm, or a serious, financial or professional setback such cooperation would be permitted.

If the nurse was engaged for a licit operation, and then, to her surprise, there is an illicit part attached to the final procedure, she would be justified in staying for the complete operation for otherwise the life of the patient might be jeopardized. As for administering the anesthesia and preparing the patient for the surgical procedure, there should be little objection for such actions are common to all surgical procedures.

In the event that the nurse is in doubt about the morality of an operation or action, she should take advice; but in case of urgency, she may trust the judgment of the doctor since it is not within her competence to judge the pathological condition of the patient. If this case presented itself with frequency, then, she would be under a more severe obligation to seek counsel, and if necessary take another position. Today, the Supreme Court would uphold the nurse's refusal to take part in any procedure that would be obnoxious to her conscience or religious convictions. Like the doctor the nurse must remember that she is a professional, a public servant, God's messenger of mercy, and in that light she must fulfill her duties.

IN EMERGENCIES

If there was ever a case wherein the moral directives of any Catholic institution would be

tested for flexibility, it is in emergencies. It is one
thing to make a decision when time is sufficient
for reflection, consultation etc. but quite another
when a decision must be made in haste. Sometimes, there are no fixed answers to a situation;
and in the medical field, developments take place
long before the Church has the occasion to render formal guidance on them.. It is in such circumstances that the good will, sincerity, moral
rectitude of the individual will have to be the
basis of the decision.

Are there any exceptions to Church doctrine
on abortion?

There are no exceptions as far as direct abortion is concerned. It is never permitted directly to
intend to empty the pregnant womb of a living
fetus before it is viable i.e., able to sustain life
outside the womb by natural or artificial means . . .

INDIRECT REMOVAL

Sometimes the life of the mother *and* of the
fetus are in jeopardy. If a fetus is doubtfully alive
in the womb, the certain right to life on the part
of the mother must prevail and the womb could
be emptied since there is no parity between a
certain right and a doubtful right.

In the case of ectopic gestation (in the fa-
lopian tubes) the situs of the fetus is not a natural
one for development. The tube is not made an-
atomically for that purpose and its condition is
considered pathological once the fetus is lodged

therein (there is an acute danger of hemorrhaging). Because it is a diseased tube, it may be removed although it contains the fetus. But care must be taken to baptize the fetus at least conditionally. The operation may be delayed as long as the delay is consistent with the mother's safety.

The same may be said if the womb is found to be cancerous during pregnancy and the excision cannot be delayed. This is not a direct attack on the life of the fetus; its death is no way intended or desired but is only an accessory consequence of a licit moral action.

The same can be said for other emergency operations on pregnant women for cases not directly involving the fetus. These may be performed even at the risk of aborting the fetus, if the need of the mother requires the operation without further delay.

DIRECT REMOVAL

Some liberal authors have the theory, that if a fetus is the basic cause of the health problems of the mother then its direct removal would be justified. For them, this action is primarily one of saving the mother's life, and the removal of the fetus only one component part of a good action. They contest the opinion that the removal of the fetus is a separate act with its own morality. This theory, as yet, is not common Church teaching.

THE LEGAL VIEWPOINT

The United States Supreme Court in January 1973 ruled that, as a subject of law, the fetus must be a real person and this is recognized as present only at birth after 9 months gestation. The fetus is held to be "viable" at the beginning of the last trimester. If born prematurely, it will be attributed personhood if and when, the characteristics of man are verified in it. But it will enjoy constitutional rights or protection only at the time of actual birth.

"The unborn child is not accorded full constitutional rights and protection until it is born; and may be slain for virtually any reason or no reason at all" (U. S. Supreme Court decision). Individual States may regulate the details of the process of abortion as long as they do not deny the actual right to abortion. This right to abortion begins at the very inception of pregnancy and continues to the time of delivery from the womb, if it is in the interest of the health and life of the mother. The Court justifies this decision on the basis of the uncertainty on the part of theologians and philosophers as to the exact moment of hominization. The Court establishes the moment of actual birth as the criterion that the fetus is human and personhood is achieved. If the Law does confer any rights on the fetus, it is in anticipation of live birth and only prevails if this is verified.

BASIS

As barbarous as the Court decision may appear it rests on three interests: the right to privacy, the State's right to protect the health of the mother, and the State's right to protect and preserve potential, human life. For the first three months of pregnancy, the right to privacy prevails and the abortion is seen as the private concern of the mother and the doctor. The second three months of pregnancy, the right of the State prevails so as to protect the life and health of the mother. The last trimester, the State vindicates primary concern for the more probable life of the fetus but not at the expense of the mother's mental or physical health.[1]

SENATOR BAYH

Senator Bayh commenting on the decision said "it is necessary to recognize that the law has been reluctant to endorse any theory that life begins before actual birth; or to assign legal rights to the unborn except in restricted, narrowly-defined situations and then only as contingent upon live birth. The Court has chosen to make prevail the life and health of the mother at all stages of pregnancy." [2]

EUROPEAN COURTS

A recent study of abortion rulings in other nations brings out important contrasts. In general, the high Courts of Austria, France, Italy, West Germany, and Canada were faced with very complex cases of abortion. Improved medical techniques, changes in sexual morality, increased sense of sexual freedom, the problem of unwanted children, fears of overpopulation and the fact of an "underresourced" world produced serious arguments favoring abortion as a means to an end. But these nations viewed relaxations of the restrictions on abortion as profoundly incompatible with the social commitment to respect the dignity of each individual human being as well as the fundamental notions of the rights of man. [3]

In their decisions, woman's right to decide to have an abortion was not recognized, in strange contrast to our Court which founded this right in the "privacy" concept of the Constitution. Furthermore, all courts except the German court, found that the right to abortion, except in an extreme case to preserve the life and health of the mother, is a legislative matter and not one for the courts to decide. They found that "everyone has the right to life" and they considered the unborn as a person. The German court declared that life exists from the 14th day after conception and this conclusion seems to have been taken as restablished by all parties. (Cf. John Marshall Law School Journal of Practice and Procedure, Chicago, 1975 — an in depth study of pro-life decision of West German Constitutional Court).

OTHER DECISIONS

Later jurisprudence clarified the original Court decision. In a federal appeals court in Kentucky, the court upheld a conscience clause in Kentucky's law which permitted medical personnel to refuse to participate in, or perform abortions on grounds of conscientious objections. It required that the mother's written permission be obtained before the child could be aborted. It ordered a 24 hour waiting period before the actual performing of the abortion, and required that the doctor inform the expectant mother of the reasonably possible physical and mental consequences of the abortion process. The same court refused to approve, or to mandate, parental or spouse's consent for the abortions to be performed on minors or wives.

On July 1, 1976 the Supreme Court ruled on a Missouri law. It ruled as unconstitutional any requirement that an unmarried minor have parental permission for an abortion, or a married person have her husband's consent. It ruled in the same sense concerning a ban on the saline amniocentesis as an abortion procedure after the first 12 weeks. It did uphold the Missouri concept of viability namely, "that stage of fetal development when the life of the unborn child may be continued indefinitely outside the womb by natural or artificial life-supportive systems." It also approved that a woman give prior written consent to an abortion; and that certain reporting and record-keeping requirements, useful to the State's interest in protecting the health of its female citizens and of medical value, be made. But, it considered invalid the proposed part of the law that would have made it obligatory on the doctor to spare no effort to save the life of the child should it survive the abortion procedure.[4]

THE VIEWS OF CONGRESS

To many in Congress, the abortion issue is a matter of concern only for the individual's conscience. They are also concerned that the law of the land should be abided by. The Supreme Court has issued its edict: to them this is a supreme norm of legal status. They feel that an amendment would meet the religious requirements of the few in contradiction to the Bill of Rights. They admit that all have the right to their own convictions and may also try to win over others to the righteousness of their views; but it is another question when a group would embody such views into a constitutional amendment since this would be an unwarranted violation of the First Amendment.

To them the dangers of legalized abortion are not real. They see no danger of compulsive abortion taking hold so that it would be practically mandatory on those who might oppose it from a conscientious viewpoint. They deny that it increases the crime of infanticide. The path to a constitutional amendment against abortion on demand, or with loose requirements, is indeed tortuous; and especially so, when the protection of the law would cover even the first moment of fertilization. Politically, some would favor protection by law but from a later period, much before actual birth.

The pro-Abortion people make statistics speak in their favor. A Gallup poll of 1972 is cited to show that 64% agreed that the decision in abortion should be left up to the mother and the doctor and that even 54% of the Catholics went along with this. The Fellows of the American College of Obstetricians and Gynecologists were 88% in favor of liberal abortion laws. In 1973 *Modern Medicine* polled its membership to find that 33,000 or 65% approved the Supreme Court's decision.[5]

OTHER VIEWPOINTS

Much has been written in theological reviews of the "preference principle" in cases of conflict of interests. Bruno Schuller would have us decide, when we are faced with two inevitable evils, which of the two is the greater and avoid it by doing the lesser. Or, in a case of conflict involving two mutually exclusive values, he would have us prefer the value of actual, dominant importance.

This "preference-principle" has evoked a great deal of discussion and could open up extraordinary difficulties. John Dedek in his fine work *"Human Life"* seems to accept the principle, if the value chosen to be preserved is proportionate to the disvalue of homicide. Writes Dedek "I would think that the only sufficient reason would be to save the physical life of the mother, or what I think to be equivalent, her mental sanity.".[1]

INCEST-RAPE CASES

In cases of rape and incest the womb of the victim could be emptied of the aggressor's seed if conception has not taken place. When does it take place? Traditional doctrine would have it happen from three to four hours after fertilization. Doctors look upon this not as an *action* but as a *process* and in general say "several hours" must elapse. Within that time after the attack, the womb may be emptied.

Other moralists take refuge in the biological-developmental theory which holds that the zygote is not irretrievably homo before the third week, and until that time, for serious personal, socioeconomic reasons would permit the emptying of the womb. Dedek cites this possibility of a solution to a difficult case[2] There are other schools of thought as to the moment that the fetus is a person, fully human.

The *Genetic School* in biology says "once conceived, the being is recognized as man simply because he has man's potential." Whoever the individual is, he is such from the first moment of conception.

The *Developmental School* agrees that conception does establish the genetic basis for an individual human being, but some degree of development is required before we can speak of an individual, a human person. How much development? This ranges from the beginning of the third week to the moment of the development of the cerebral cortex whereby self awareness is achieved — possibly around the sixth month. Many of this school would tell us to be more concerned with human persons and not simply with human life as the criterion for banning abortions, but one can easily see the hazards of this line of thought.

The *Social-Consequences School* is the most liberal. It claims that biological evidence leaves us free to draw a line between human (person) and non-human as we wish, at least up to a very liberal period of time; so in a critical situation we should avail ourselves of that liberty to serve our social needs as best we can.

Abortion should be made available to those who want or need it, without any moral recriminations, up to the time the child has the capacity to relate inter-personally, build culture on its part and think. Such capacities might not be even had at the time of viability! Outstanding proponents of this school agree that biologically a fertilized ovum is a potential human being but only in the narrowest sense of the term; genetically, after the 8th week, morphologically, it may have human characteristics; but the real human being thinks, inter-relates.

This theory is held to be very dangerous since "humans" are judged humans on the basis of their social usefulness — what would prevent easy abortion, infanticide, and mercy killing of the chronically-ill, the senile and the habitual criminal?

This school's philosophical orientation is adopted by so many of our contemporaries and it would seem that the majority opinion of the Supreme Court, in its basic decision on abortion, was based on such premises. The Church opinion comes closer to the Genetic school; and among Catholic authors, a modified Developmental school philosophy prevails.[3]

CATHOLICS – PRO ABORTION?

Somtimes, much is made of the sympathy of some Catholics for liberalized abortion laws. It cannot be denied that the general laxity in the area of morals, and particularly on the theme of sex, has made inroads into Catholic positions and made many less opposed to the crime of abortion. But, in all fairness, we should not take the 1973 poll ,conducted under the auspices of the National Opinion Research Center along religious affiliation lines to be indicative of abortion-attitudes, without some reservations. The Catholic respondents did give limited approval: they approved of it under limited circumstances and not simply permissive abortion for any reason or for none at all. Thus, 88% were in favor if the mother's health was in jeopardy; 75% would permit it in cases of rape; 77% would permit it if the child was going to be born a defective child. If the child was going to be unwanted, 34% would permit abortion similarly if the mother was unwed, or too poor, to have another child, 39%.

Reading the statistics we can see how true is the statement "the right to life is no longer a right but is dependent on the comfort and well-being of the mother." (Senator Bartlett). For far too many, the unborn's right to life is limited and secondary to that of the mother even to the moment of actual birth. The Supreme Court canonized this mentality. For Catholics to dedicate themselves to the strict norm of protection of the unborn from the first moment of conception will mean a fierce loyalty on their part to God and His Church. The Church fights for respect of human life, at any and all stages of development; secular opinon calls for respect and legal protection for the person, and does not see the fetus as a person, most frequently until actual birth. For some Catholics, it is easily presumed, this is indeed a hard saying.[4]

HUMAN EXPERIMENTATION

One of the most sensitive areas in medical practice is that which pertains to research. Unless research is permitted, unless the unknown is explored, unless new drugs, new procedures are experimented with, and the side effects and concomitant risks endured, mankind will remain heir to the most devastating diseases. The dilemma is always "how far can we go into human experimentation to expand medical knowledge and still protect the dignity and security of the human person"? Theologians clamor for controls, effective and efficient, on human experimentation. God's image in every human calls for respect and reverence as much in this area as that of abortion.

This area of medical practice has made enormous strides in past years and greater progress is promised in the near future. Scientists predict that soon a man will be made to order! His sex will be predetermined, his I.Q. will match his psychical and physical make-up; the color of his skin and eyes will be a problem of simple choice. Test-tube babies are a possibility; some claim they have already been made. But with all this, scientists are disturbed for as Dr. Muller, a Nobel Prize winner says "if man does not directly control the process of genetic transmission, the natural resource of human heredity, man's pool of genetic material, will become so polluted with defensive genes, that within a few more generations, the world will be over-populated with people who will have serious genetic defects."

CONDITIONS

In experimentations on humans, it is first required, by reason of human dignity, that the subject give informed approval, i.e., that the subject know the risks involved, and willingly assume them. The ideal image would be that the doctor and the patient form a partnership in the project and both share the responsibility and glory. The experimentation may be therapeutic, i.e., done with the hope of some advantage accruing to the subject. In this case, informed consent is required and consideration must be given to other factors such as the chances of success, the cost, etc. and unless these are reasonable, the project would be useless, possibly harmful. In all cases, the subject must be accorded the right to die with dignity and under no pretext be kept alive by extraordinary means.

When the experiment is non-therapeutic, i.e., the subject will probably receive no benefit but will enable others to benefit from what is learned, no one has the right to impose the experiment, and the informed consent of the subject is more imperative than in the former hypothesis, and under the same conditions and with a real need in view. If the subject is unable to give consent, then his next of kin should be asked. This is a laudable way to affirm one's love for Christ in neighbor and concern for others by submitting to experiments for the betterment of mankind but does not oblige under serious inconvenience or pain etc. We must avoid in this domain two extremes: excessive individualism and egotism which begets no concern at all for others; and the totalitarian concept that the individual is there to be the guinea pig of the community; that he is the property of the State.[5]

GENETIC COUNSELING

Genetic counseling seems to be very advisable today in cases wherein genetic defects are known to be prone to appear. It is common knowledge that Jewish people are subject to the Toy-Sachs syndrome and the Blacks to that of the sickle-cell anemia. A good many such defects can be detected today by the process of amniocentesis, i.e., a sample of the fluid from the bag of water surrounding the fetus is taken and examined. It is true that some abuse this procedure for doing away with the fetus but it is also very useful in helping to detect and then cure the defect. Today, the entire field of Fetology is involved in trying to assure each child of a healthy entrance into the world. We read of sperm-banks, artificial insemination, transfer of ovaries, vast medical research into the realm of injurious syndromes protection of the fetus from "rubela" etc. The field is not only vast but complex and requires professional specialization. It behooves each one to be aware of what is being done and be able to evaluate some of the procedures from a moral viewpoint.

LATEST REPORT

The official National Commission for the Protection of Subjects of Biomedical and Behavioral Research was established in 1974, to study policies under which research could be carried out and supported particularly in the domain of fetal research; it also was to set forth the ethical principles which would guide experimentation on the embryo. On June 12, 1975 its report was filed as to the ethical, medical, juridical aspects of human experimentation. Msgr. J. McHugh of the NCCB's office praised its work for it did seem to protect the dignity of the human fetus. Fr. McCormick was pleased with the equal protection given to all fetuses. But. Dr. Hellegers of the Kennedy Institute partially accepted the recommendations on the research on the fetus in the womb but found unsatisfactory what was said about experimentation on the fetus outside the womb. Dr. David Louisell acknowledged the many fine points in the report, but on the question of non-therapeutic research as to the fetus in anticipation of it being aborted, and what was permitted on the fetus aborted, yet living, he was strongly in opposition.

FETAL RESEARCH

The fetus is not able to respond for itself so consent by proxy is necessary when experimentation is contemplated. It may be presumed in the case of therapeutic research when there are benefits as well as risks in it for the fetus itself. But proxy consent in case of non-therapeutic research is much more difficult to justify.

For therapeutic consent, the mother and father may give proxy consent; the father's refusal is equivalent to a veto of the project. In non-therapeutic experimentation more urgent reasons seem to be required.

When the research is done on a pregnant woman with risk possible to the fetus, the woman's consent is sufficient, if the risks are kept to the minimum and proportionate care assured for the woman. When no advantage is to accrue to either the mother or the fetus, proxy consent is sufficient if the risks are kept to a minimum; the mother alone can give the consent, if the father does not object; and the same norms apply as to the risks for the fetus whether it is to be aborted or not. This principle of equality for the fetuses was openly controverted from a pragmatic viewpoint since a good many of the members felt that procedures that would not be used on a fetus destined for full term, could be used if the fetus was to be aborted. It was agreed that in cases of disagreement, these would be subject to review at a national level. But the mother's consent in either case is required; it was disputed whether the father should have any say in non-therapeutic research directed toward the woman.

If research is done during the abortion procedure, the subject (fetus) is dying, and therefore, the risk element is of little importance and the mother has no chance of changing her mind as to the act; but nevertheless, the commission opted for the highest respect for the dignity of the fetus and no therapeutic procedures are permissible which would alter the duration of the life of the non-viable fetus ex utero.

If the fetus should be older than was presumed, there is a moral and legal obligation to attempt to save the life of a possibly-viable infant (although a very recent decision by the Supreme Court voided the obligation on the part of the doctor to do all in his power to save the fetus).

The Commission adopted unanimously this recommendation: "No individual shall be required to perform or assist in the performance of any part of a health service, program or research activity, funded in whole or in part by the Health, Education and Welfare Dept., if his performance or assistance would be contrary to his religious beliefs or moral convictions." [6]

Linacre Quarterly, May 1976, p. 73 has a splendid article by William E. May who disagrees with above provisions in non-therapeutic procedures: "I believe that proxy consent in such cases is morally unjustifiable ..." He feels that children and incompetents are not charged with the responsibility to contribute to the general benefit and that their moral worth and integrity should be protected against any such intrusion.

THE VIEWS OF UNIVERSITY PRESIDENTS

The Presidents of two Catholic universities spoke about the Church's interest in public policies and, in particular, on the subject of abortion.

Rev. Donald Merrifield of Loyola Marymount, in Los Angeles in a symposium at Notre Dame University on Jan. 11, 1976 chose as his topic "The Worldliness of Catholicism" in which he meant to convey the full variety of interactions between Catholic belief, traditions and the world in which Catholicism has lived and grown. He stressed the important role the higher centers of learning play in American life both religious and secular; but, in particular, he declared that Catholic Universities should be characterized by intellectual reflection, integrative of and open to, the fulness of human experience, always faithful to the basic, ultimate question. Universities especially Catholic affiliated should encourage responsible criticism upon all aspects of society; they should teach their students to question and to judge issues and be afired with an ardent commitment against the destructive, the oppressive, the inhuman; and if "our education does not make an impact on the values of our graduates, especially on their social values, then, we should indeed go out of business"! (Cf. Origins, Sept. 30, 1976, p. 234).

FR. TIMOTHY HEALY, S.J.

The new president of Georgetown uttered the same principles and desires for social action on the part of the Universities and the students. But he warned that the Church must not become a one-issue people lest it lose its ability to stay in the political arena. There must be no doubt that the Church has the right to be in that arena and argue its cause without ambiguity. Speaking about abortion he added "the option of death is always terrible and offensive both to the sacred and the secular traditions in which we live. The Church's fight against it is both a natural and a healthy instinct. How can we best alert all men to see the danger ahead? It is at this point that we pass from morality to the public policy stage and it is here that anger and emotions can displace reasonable discussion. For the latter the University must always speak."

Fr. Healy reminds us that it would be a serious mistake to be a one-issue Church and to reduce all political issues to that one issue not only in major political contests, but in local politics. He reminds us that "voters who respond to only one issue are leashed to it and by one yank they all fall in line." He added that Catholic office-holders cannot survive in a political, one issue-world and the danger for the Church in these circumstances stems from its possible identification with one party, one candidate, one political strategy. As a result of this, millions of Catholics will not accept such identification for they care too much for their church to see it "hobbled" to a political stake. He asks "what deeper risk is there than to risk the Church's ability to remain in the political arena, where for the good of the Republic it surely must remain, and not only remain but remain active?"

Pleading for reasonable discussion and understanding on all sides, Fr. Healy asks "for all our learning, have we cared enough for either of the great powers which we are bound to love and serve, to see the clear imperative their opposition lays on us? . . . to see the same God manifesting His power everywhere and on both sides? Above all, do we at Georgetown see our university as a place where these powers themselves can discover the same God in each other?"

Fr. Healy ends on a lofty tone "God made the angels to show His splendor . . . but man He made to serve him wittily in the tangle of his mind! If He suffers us to fall to such a case that there is no escaping, then we stand to our tackle as best we can . . . and no doubt God is delighted to see splendor where he looked only for complexity. But it is God's part, not our own, to bring ourselves to that extremity!" (R. Bolt's "Man For all Seasons," Sir Thomas More speaks. CF.: Origins, Sept. 30, 1976: The Abortion Debate and Catholic Universities, p. 232).

ABORTION AND FUTURE PREGNANCIES

Eastern Europe, England, Israel, Japan have done vast research on the problem: does an abortion affect the future pregnancies of the subject? Our country has just begun to fund such research so that "we do not know at this present time" is the answer to the question insofar as it pertains to the United States. (Dept. of Health and Welfare and Education Report). In general, the studies show that previously-induced abortions greatly multiply the long-term risks of miscarriage, premature deliveries, abnormal pregnancies, birth defects and infant mortality. These complications are attributed to the injury and infection of the uterine lining to which the fetus adheres and also to the damage done the cervix during the process of the abortion.

Dr. Kotasek of Charles Univeristy in Prague declared that only 57% of post abortion pregnancies were found to carry to full term; and of that number, miscarriages were observed 2.2 times more often than in pregnant women without a history of abortion. After one abortion, chances of prematurity increased 40% and after two or more, the odds rose to 70% and greater. Ectopic pregnancies were twice as frequent in women who had had abortions and one clinic reported a 130% increase of these conditions after legalization of abortion. Poland had incidences of abnormal pregnancies and Japan indicated congenital birth defects increased. Israel found early deaths of the new-born doubled while later deaths of the neonatal were three and four times higher. (Cf. Moneyworth, Oct. 11, 1976, pp. 1 and 10).

PART 3

CONTRACEPTION

Questions about the nonprocreative dimension of marital love have flooded moral theology literature and the minds of men for the past twenty years in a marked degree. The values of sex have been widely discussed due perhaps to the throes of the sexual revolution, to the unheard-of liberty in the area of sex and morals, and to the irresponsible flaunting of the subject in the communication media. Instead of studying the values of marriage, it seemed that the emphasis was on the enjoyment of sensual pleasure without any thought of the obligations attached to the use of the generative faculty.

The personal fulfillment and happiness of married life soon was affected by this secularistic mentality on sex. Many couples felt a frustration in their marital life. Lack of openness and of appreciation for the concrete values of human love robbed them of a deep responsible affection without which marriage cannot thrive. If conjugal love does not embrace a complete giving of self on the part of both partners and if, along with this gift, there is not that unselfish devotion of persons and complete surrender of bodies then personal fulfillment from a love which is undying and essentially oriented to a sharing in God's creativity in the transmission of life, will have been missed and with it, the genius of Christian marriage.

Many reproach the Christian concept of marriage and its love as being too spiritual. It is true that the love characteristic of conjugal love would well be named 'erotic love.' But this love is not purely sexual or physical or spiritual. Granted that the stress is on the physical, conjugal love must embrace all three loves: the love of friendship, the love of agape-concern, deep interest — and finally, erotic love the desire for physical contact and union. It is true that conjugal love is a mixture of all three but its main thrust, in a sense, is self-gratification; it is 'self-directed.' But in a very human way, it is also 'other-directed and we might describe it as "We love us." The dignity of the human person uplifts the sensual and erotic.

Herbert Richardson in his *Nun, Witch, Playmate* writes "when yoked to love, sensuality is concerned with the transformation of Eros, a sensual love, to Agape, and the unselfish giving love." And Michael Valenti, in *The Radical Vision of a Catholic Theologian* adds "Eros, whilst retaining all its natural force, becomes agape i.e. the expression of a love which is essentially oriented to God, a love of two Christians with all that this implies."

But if Eros does not take that step and the partners of marriage stay within the goal of self-seeking and self-gratification, then Eros will lead to the shirking of the duty of love-outgoing, and procreation will be given no place. Catholic theology on Marriage has never sanctioned pleasure for pleasure's sake. Eros always has had to satisfy a primary or secondary end in marriage. Perhaps that is the reason why today the Catholic doctrine on Contraception has caused and is causing such a furore in world so self-seeking and egocentric.

WHAT IT IS

Contraception is the employment of any mechanical, chemical or other means (including the interruption of the act of intercourse) to hinder the conception of new human life. Avoiding generation by abstention from intercourse is not contraception.

Each new generation of people finds this a new problem but in fact it has been with the Church from the earliest times, varying from extreme libertarianism (totally separating intercourse from procreation) to an extreme asceticism (prohibiting procreation altogether!). This was within the Church. Outside the Church, of course, the pagan world was notoriously careless of human life and such practices as abandoning children to beasts of prey, infanticide and similar destruction of incipient life were common.

Reacting to these challenges, the Church has consistently defended the importance of procreation and prohibited any interference with the act by which life is transmitted. From the thirteenth century to the eighteenth her views were substantially the norm for Christian people. But, early in the nineteenth century, the views of Malthus became more widely accepted in England and France and birth prevention was presented as the remedy for the social ills of those days. Towards the end of that century the problem became acute and has remained so since, especially following the introduction of sophisticated birth-prevention methods particularly the contraceptive pill.

THE   JUDEO-CHRISTIAN   VIEWPOINT

Up to 1930 there was practical unanimity among Jews and non-Jews concerning contraception. There was agreement that Genesis 38, v. 7 (the sin of Onan) constituted a strict prohibition of artificial birth prevention procedures.

In the remote past, there was common acceptance of the axiom that the rights of the individual in human sexuality should yield to the superior right of society, so that the use of sex always was oriented to the preservation of the race in its basic unity, the family. The primary end of marriage was held to be the procreation and education of offspring. Then followed the good of the spouses, with their harmony and need of affection. St. Augustine's ordering of the good of marriage has received monotonous repetition: *proles, fides, sacramentum*. The *debitum* (conjugal duties) loomed as an important part of the marriage contract because it assured and protected the primacy of the offspring in the conjugal union.

PIUS XI

Pius XI in his otherwise severe *Casti Connubii* (1931) declared that an ethic of love between the spouses was as essential to the proper ordering of marriage as its orientation to procreation. After this encouragement, manuals began to stress the personalistic values of marriage. Dr. Don Dominian was one of the first with his *The Meaning and Ends of Marriage*. For him, the meaning of the sex act was first and foremost the union of two persons which found its highest expression in the manner the spouses gave themselves one to another physically.

Pope Pius XII said that Christian spouses were persons, and that sex was more than a biological action. Said the Pope "to reduce the cohabitation of married people and the conjugal act to mere organic function for the transmission of the germ of life, would be to convert the domestic hearth, the sanctuary of the family, into nothing more than a biological laboratory . . . the conjugal act is a personal action, a simultaneous mutual self-giving, which in the words of Holy Scripture, effects the union in flesh."

THE "PILL"

After World War II, Moralists clamored for a re-orientation of the doctrine on Christian Marriage. This was the era of sex revolution when idols of the past were crashing fast to the ground — authority, government-mandates, life styles and the stability of the home. The 'Pill' was discovered as a response to the challenge of checking population growth from the multiplicity of youthful marriages and libertine sex morals. The debate continued until 1968 as to whether intercourse was to serve personal fulfillment independently or necessarily in conjunction with the procreation of offspring.

VATICAN II

Vatican II purposely omitted the division of 'primary and secondary ends' in marriage. It called marriage a 'community of love' for personal growth and mature fulfillment but withal, a community by nature oriented to procreation. It gave the parents the right to determine the size of their families, it acknowledged that circumstances might impose a curtailment in its size. But the Council did declare "by their very nature, the institutions of marriage along with true conjugal love are ordained essentially for the procreation and education of children and find in this their ultimate crown."

Procreation must never be the sole consideration in marriage but it is an essential characteristic of the institution. Vatican II acknowledged the traditional ends of marriage but put them in better focus. Fr. John Fox who was present at the Council wrote that the Council did not intend to prejudge the meaning and the hierarchy of the ends of marriage. It neither intended to reject them or affirm them — but to leave them in abeyance.

The Council did admit the possibility of delaying procreation at least temporarily due to circumstances. It sensed that the question of the transmission of life had to be clarified. It did not attempt to describe any specific method of birth-regulation since Pope Paul had notified it that he had reserved the question for his own personal study. It did, however, state that the guidelines for man's sexual conduct should be based on man's *person* and on the *nature of rational actions*.

HUMANAE VITAE

After long and personal study, Pope Paul VI rejected the findings of the Papal Commission on Birth Control, and then gave to the world his answer to the problem of the transmission of life and its regulation in marriage: *Humanae Vitae*.

The central message of this document is expressed: *every contraceptive act is intrinsically evil because every marital act must be open to the transmission of new life*. Intercourse is envisaged as a single act with two inner meanings: the unitive and the procreative. By divine design these two meanings are inseparable. Anyone who attempts to make intercourse sterile, attacks the very essence of it, as an expression of mutual self-giving. The Pope declared that this doctrine had the sanction of Natural Law.

The physical structure of the act of intercourse makes it unitive and procreative at one and the same time: they are inseparable. It unites the couple but also capacitates them to generate new life. Intercourse is an expression of conjugal love but is simultaneously a call to parenthood. The latter must always be honored, at least by implicit intent. Man cannot separate the unitive from the procreative aspect because man has no dominion over the generative powers. The physiological structure of the sexual act, in the Pope's view, determines its use, meaning and morality.

The Pope was constrained to reject the conclusions of the Commission on Birth Control primarily because "they had grave implications for other questions — neither slight nor few — of a doctrinal as well as of a pastoral and social nature . . ." Besides, "certain criteria for solutions had emerged from the Commission's judgment which departed from the moral teachings on marriage proposed with constant firmness by the teaching authority of the Church."

The document maintained that the problem of contraception had new aspects and it reaffirmed the competency of the Magisterium on the point since Jesus Christ had constituted the Pope and Bishops, as successors of the Apostles, "guardians and authentic interpreters of the moral law, not only that of the Law of the Gospel but also of the Natural Law."

The Holy Father realized that responsible parenthood sometimes calls for regulation of births. He referred to Vatican II which calls Marriage a divine institution wherein husband and wife, by reciprocal mutual gift of self, bind themselves in a communion of being and love for the attainment of mutual, personal perfection through the full expression of a human love that is physical, spiritual, total, faithful, exclusive and fruitful. They collaborate with God Himself in the act of procreation.

This conjugal love is oriented to a truly human fecundity which takes into consideration the personal viewpoints of the spouses and engenders in them a true awareness of responsible parenthood. In light of the latter, decisions will be made as to the size of the family. Sometimes abstention or continence for an indeterminate period of time or the delay of a new birth will be in order. But in all times and in all decisions, responsible parenthood will impose respect for the *objective moral* order established by God.

Humanae Vitae clearly prohibits deliberate contraception in any form since it conflicts with the biological laws which are part of the human person. The Pope also calls attention to the *assistance of the Holy Spirit* in arriving at this decision and to the Magisterium of the Church even when it is a question of a non infallible decision. The document is an authentic pronouncement of the Teaching Church, merits full and loyal assent both interior and exterior and, in spite of dissenting views which are detailed in subsequent pages, makes it very difficult to justify a *probable* opinion contrary to its teaching.

THE   MEDICAL   VIEWPOINT

Contraception is a problem of no small magnitude for the individual, as well as for society. It is one thing to outline it, quite another to ask ourselves what is being done to solve it

LICIT MEANS

Abstention during the fertile period in the woman's monthly cycle is known as **Rhythm.** This is the use of intercourse during the two sterile portions of the menstrual cycle, with abstention during the fertile period.

The theory is based on the fact that the ovum is released 12 to 16 days before the next period of menstruation. For the average woman, this happens within two weeks or so but the safer range is between 12 to 16 days. The unfertilized ovum will live a maximum of 72 hours. If there is double ovulation this takes place within 24 hours of the first.

To make success in the method more probable, take the time of ovulation, add 2 days before that date for the possible life of sperm in the body and another two or three days after the ovulation ends. This gives the fertile days with a high degree of accuracy.

Mathematically, this is the situation: a normal cycle from menstruation to menstruation is 28 days. Count back 16 days (from 28th) and add two more days for the life of possible sperm in the body. This gives the *beginning* of ovulation. Counting back 12 days gives the *end* of the period but, since the ovum could come toward the end, we add another 2 days for this contingency. This brings us to nine days before the next menstruation. Those who are successful with the method make their abstention time from day 19 to day 9 before menstruation.

Since the menstrual cycle varies in length even normally, it is advised that we combine the Rhythm with the **Temperature method.** This would include the taking of the temperature the first thing in the morning upon rising. For the first seven or ten days of the month it will remain on the lower level. For three to seven days it will rise and this rise will indicate that the period of ovulation has begun and that the fertile period is open.

It will soon be patent after a month or two that a definite pattern is verified as to this monthly rise. It is true that illness or any physical disturbance, during the night, will affect the degree but doctors are certain that an hour's rest before the taking of the temperature will correct the possible variation. This method is extremely easy to apply, and if the person knows her basic menstrual cycle, will greatly aid to confirm it.

Another easy method of knowing when the ovulation period begins is through the presence of **glucose** in the cervix. This is verified just before, during, and for a little while after the process of ovulation. It is there to aid the longevity of the sperm. Fertility tape enables the woman to test for it. Pink tape will turn to a heavy blue at the beginning and as the days of ovulation pass the blue will gradually lighten and disappear; when the tape remains its normal pink, for 3 days, then, ovulation is terminated.

Again it is counseled to use this method in conjunction with the temperature process.

The **Billings Method** of establishing the moment of ovulation is rather intricate, demanding strict and careful observation on the part of the woman. It is based on a change in the thickness of vaginal body secretions. As ovulation is about to take place the secretion takes on something akin to the thickness or density of the fluid part of a raw egg. As ovulation terminates, the density of the secretions becomes less and less till the next menstruation arrives.

Further research is being carried on with some encouragement, but sufficient funds are lacking. Dr. John Rock, famous for his discovery of the "Pill" tells us that if the funds were available, existing laboratory techniques could be perfected and simplified so that the average woman, in the privacy of her bedroom, could easily and safely forecast and pinpoint ovulation. (cf *Sex Fertility, and the Catholic* by the Kanabays, p 138). Georgetown University's Center for Population Research is conducting a nationwide study to perfect the Rhythm method. A new product "Estrindex" manufactured by Colab, of Chicago Heights, may yet help to determine exact dates by diagnosing the concentration of salt in a woman's body, because the salt increases in quantity prior to and at the time of ovulation.

ILLICIT MEANS

Illicit means of birth regulation and control are many and varied. Usually they are designed to thwart the act of intercourse by placing an artificial barrier between the sperm and the ovum, by using some extrinsic device such as a condom or occlusive pessary or by destroying the viability of the spermatozoa with spermicidal douches or jellies.

Today considerable investigation is taking place to induce contraception pharmacologically and this will be brought about by the suppression or modification of the endocrine processes essential to reproduction. A physiologic pattern hostile to ovulation is created. Perhaps the generic name for all this would be "The Pill": all compounds of various progestational ingredients. These could be contraceptive but they can be used also for testing ovarian function, correction of menstrual disorders, and the preventing of abortive pregnancies. Doctors have had success through these medications in treating various disorders. Used as a medication, there is no moral objection. Used as a contraceptive, these procedures would be immoral. When the intent is righteous, the side effects of temporary sterilization must be tolerated to obtain a cure seriously needed. The doctor should make the patient well aware of some of the side effects from a constant usage of these compounds.

Jellies, creams, and foams whilst they leave the physical structure of the act of intercourse intact, do destroy the vitality of the male spermatozoa and are thus contraceptive and immoral.

The IntraUterine Device is immoral, because "women wearing intrauterine devices do ovulate and can conceive. But, most of the time the fertilized ovum may fail to implant because it reaches the uterus before its invasive ability is fully developed, or before endometrial changes have advanced enough to receive it. There is also the possibility that an intrauterine device can alter stromal development enough to make it unsuitable for implantation" (cf O'Donnell, T. J.: *Medicine and Christian Morality*, p 246).

The Morning-after-pill is identified as an abortifacient because it prevents implantation after destroying a fertilized ovum (and new life is presumed to be present from the moment of fertilization). The surgical process of Dilation and Curettage (D and C) after rape looks like abortion since it will result in preventing implantation of an embryo.

Permanent sterilization via a surgical operation of tubal (bilateral) ligation or vasectomy and with contraceptive intent is morally wrong. Until the victim sincerely repents and is forgiven, marital intercourse would be immoral because the contraceptive distortion continues. Must the person undergo a second operation to restore his generative potential? The surgical technique for this is not, as yet, looked upon as successful or without a degree of danger. It would be difficult to impose such an operation.

THE MORAL VIEWPOINT

The moral viewpoint on Contraception has already been partly stated in previous pages dealing with *Humanae Vitae*. Here we briefly summarize the principal reactions to that document in 1968 and how thinking has since developed.

The morality, or otherwise, of contraception is closely linked to the concept of what is called "Natural Law." By this is meant a Law or Rule of action implicit in a thing's very nature. It can refer to organic or inorganic activities but is particularly applied to human beings and describes a rule of conduct proper to them.

To be sure that we are correctly interpreting and unfolding the Law, we must call upon human reason and gather all that science, experiences, experts and insights into man's behavior can tell us about the body and the social side of man. The conclusions drawn from these sources should be evident to all, open to all and easily grasped by all.

They should be intelligible to the better-educated but should equally represent what should be done, or is done by rational people when they are enabled to choose freely.

In the massing of evidence the margin of error is large. A constant check must be maintained on the search for truth. This does not mean any disrespect for legitimate authority nor does it derogate from its powers. Rather the purpose is to aid the authority in making correct decisions.

Christ gave all things their final value and new "birth." The latter penetrates the "whole man." The morality inspired by Christ's love for man, and His revelation, not only differs *quantitatively* but *qualitatively* from the morality of mere natural law aided by revelation.

The Church is mandated to form a world according to the Christian view and she should be a recognized source of the unfolding of the Natural Law through experience and reflections. Most assuredly, the Church is a source when she compares the Natural Law with Revelation and when she supervises and criticizes its directives.

Since Christ's influence is suffused in man's understanding of himself, the competence of the Church is deeply involved in the concrete applications of the Natural Law to every life. When she does apply it, this is done as a living re-evaluation of the meaning Christ gave to human life.

The Church is aided in her task by the assistance of the Holy Spirit especially in the amassing of evidence, experiences and data on which to base her decisions. Man is expected to aid the Spirit in this work. Failure to make a thorough search for truth means that the Spirit may be unable to make the correct meaning evolve. The presumption is always in favor of the Spirit's having received sufficient human co-operation, but each case has to be taken on its merits and it is useful to remember that those who do not accept current Church teaching on contraception, base at least part of their case on what they feel was inadequate human research.

As against this opinion, we must keep in mind the perfection the Church brings to the interpretation of the "pure and simple" directives of Natural Law. What seems to us just an *ideal* may be what the Father requires of *all Christians* whom he has called to be as perfect as He is.

REACTION TO HUMANAE VITAE

When the history of Moral Theology in the 20th century is written, *Humanae Vitae* will be recognized as THE important document; and Pope Paul may well be hailed as a prophet who cried out for greater integrity of the spouses in the fulfillment of their marital duties, and for the world to regard human sexuality with reverence and respect and noble intent. The ideal proposed by this prophet, as to the transmission of new life in each and every act of conjugal sex, is indeed a heavy burden for married couples to assume because of their own moral weakness, the materialistic culture in which they live and the economic hardships of modern living. Like all prophets, Pope Paul had a perspective totally different from that of his listeners.

The Episcopal Conferences of the world sensed the righteousness of the ideal set before all men by the non-infallible magisterium on the subject of birth regulation. At the same time, they were very cognizant of the burden that faced all engaged in the pastoral ministry. They felt concern for the faithful and the problems of their local churches in the loyal acceptance of the doctrine in all its purity. They exhorted their faithful to a spirit of filial love and obedience to the Holy Father. Few exacted absolute and immediate obedience.

The hierarchies of Canada, the United States, Belgium, and France recognized the right and duty of honest research and reflection on the proposal with the consequent right to withhold assent, if the individual sincerely felt constrained to do so. Dissenters could have arguments to justify their position contrary to the teaching, but these had to be held and published with good will, with respect for Papal teaching authority, and with all danger of scandal removed.

The Bishops were also cognizant of the conflicts that might arise in the carrying out of the teachings in every day life from the viewpoint of health and economics. Continence, too, could threaten family peace and even the life of the marriage. The Belgian, Canadian, Indonesian, French, Swiss and East German Hierarchies were agreed that such spouses in conflict should ponder "that the Church demands that they loyally seek a manner of acting which would enable them to adapt their conduct to their vows as prescribed. If they cannot, all at once, then, they should not consider themselves separated from God." Confession and Communion were counselled as remedies and as aids for gradual acceptance of Papal teaching.

The Bishops of Liege, and Namur (Belgium) declared "in conflict of duties, one chooses that value which presents itself as higher in the scale of duties even though the choice involves the renunciation of others."

The Indonesians admitted that, in a particular case, in order to safeguard the mutual love and welfare of a family, man and wife could well come to a decision which would differ from that of the Encyclical.

The French hierarchy gave the most nuanced statement. Contraception, they said, is never good. It is always a disorder, although not always culpable. In a real conflict of duties, one must choose certain obligations, in circumstances sometimes that no matter what one chooses, evil cannot be avoided.

Partners before God will determine which duties are to prevail in an emergency. This will denote a responsible, well-informed conscience.

Even though the Bishops did recognize the pastoral need to adjust the teaching, at least temporarily, and in conflict, there was no hesitancy, or at least doubt, in their own minds; they surely had no difficulty in accepting the Pope's teaching. The German, French, Belgian and United States Episcopates maintained that this teaching was an authentic, non-infallible teaching of the Magisterium. As such it merited a religious obedience to its findings and a submission of will and mind primarily based on the religious motivation to which the Church, sacramentally instituted, appeals. The assistance of the Holy Spirit commands our filial loyalty. The force of the arguments adduced to bolster the teaching were to be considered as of partial consequence. The Bishops agreed that the Church had the authority and the duty to confirm the moral order founded on human nature itself (Germans); or to interpret the Natural Law (Belgians); or to declare the meaning of the Natural Law (Cardinal O'Boyle).

As to freedom to dissent: the Bishops could not forbid it, but they were not without some apprehension. The German bishops admitted its possibility in a theoretical sense; but warned their faithful that they should examine well their consciences before coming to the conclusion of dissenting, so that they could render an account of this serious act before God. The Belgian Bishops reasoned in the same vein.

EXCEPTIONS

The Hierarchies did not make mention of any disagreement with the basics of the Encyclical, but their willingness to concede the theoretical possibility of dissent, and the indulgence which they showed in principle with those who might find themselves in conflict give rise to the presumption that some of the bishops might have sensed a rigor of judgment in the teaching. Failure to avoid something intrinsically evil was tolerated. On what score? For those in sincere dissent, their good faith made them see no evil in their action. For those in conflict who were not in theoretical dissent, what?

Some writers justify a decision contrary to the teaching of the Pope by saying that no action is *intrinsically evil* until it has been placed in the *context of real life*; and then and then only can it be judged from the intent and circumstances inherent in it.

Others would say that a disorder may be *tolerated* for greater benefits equally vital due to circumstances.

Others justify the toleration of an intrinsic disorder on the basis of the nature of the Papal teaching: the Pope enunciated a *general principle* and let the Bishops make the applications in concrete individual cases. These writers draw a contrast between this and the principle 'thou shalt not kill' of the Natural Law. The latter is a general principle; it needs refinement since there is no provision in it for killing in self defense.

As to the precept that every act of conjugal sex must be left open to the transmission of new life: this is the general principle and is true in itself. It is now up to the Bishops to determine *refinements* of the principle, and cases in which it does not apply. They point out that the Papal Commission on birth control declared that contraception would be sinful *only in* the case of a selfish, egotistical way of married life in which *any* creative opening to the family would be refused.

OTHER   VIEWPOINTS

The cultural and religious background of **Eastern religions** does not favor contraception. Hindus, Buddhists and Muslims look upon birth prevention as an affront to personal probity and physical modesty. Tribal traditions and customs frown upon it.

In the **Judeo Christian** tradition, the most telling break was that of the Church of England. In 1930 the Lambeth Conference made a distinction to the effect that abstinence was the preferred method of birth regulation; but if this mode failed or was found to be impractical, impossible, or untrustworthy, then other contraceptive methods were to be permitted. This permissive attitude was soon followed by others. The Committee on Marriage and the Home decided for the Federated Churches in the United States that it was permissible to use contraceptives in a careful, restrained manner. This became the rule for all churches except the fundamentalist groups.

In 1930 the Central Conference of American Reformed Rabbis approved contraception for economic, social and health reasons. The Rabbinical Conservative Assembly did the same in 1935 and were followed by the Orthodox in 1958 but the latter branch approved it only for health and family reasons.

After the publication of *Humanae Vitae* the Lambeth Conference praised Paul VI for his deep concern for the integrity of Christian married life but stated: "we were unable to agree with the Pope's conclusion that all methods of contraception other than total abstinence from sexual intercourse, or its confinement to periods of infecundity, are contrary to the order established by God.

Marriage is a vocation from God to holiness wherein man and woman share the love and creative purpose of God. It is true that self indulgence and (gross) sensuality destroy the true nature of the relationship of the spouses for sexual love is not an end in itself, nor is it for pure self gratification.

The responsibility for the number of children and the frequency of childbirth is laid by God on the consciences of the parents. They must make the choice before God and their wise stewardship of their resources and abilities and thought of population needs and problems of society should indicate the proper approach to procreative responsibilities" (cf. Theological Studies Dec. 1968 p. 597).

BEFORE THE POPE SPOKE

It is worthwhile to survey the consensus of theologians on contraception *before* the Encyclical *Humanae Vitae* appeared and *after*. Many, before 1968, held that the doctrine on contraception was in a state of practical doubt and open to solution via "probabilism". (*A view that any solidly probable course may be followed, even if another is or appears to be more probable.*)

In June of 1964 Pope Paul declared in one of his allocutions: "we frankly say that we do not, *so far*, see any reason for considering the relevant norms of Pius XII superceded, and therefore, no longer obligatory. We do not feel obliged to modify them." Pope Pius XII had been speaking about oral contraception. "So far" would denote that the question was under study. This statement was not—of course—an authentic, official teaching.

On Oct. 29, 1966 Pope Paul spoke on the subject of contraception and its morality when he assured us that a decision would be forthcoming but "that the traditional norms on the subject were the most sacred and the best for everybody, and that these were constituted by the law of God rather than by our authority." This again was not an official, authentic teaching but a shadow of things to come.

Before that, on Feb. 26, 1966, the Pope spoke about the Papal Commission on Birth Control and its work and said that a response could not be given as yet because a study had to make it certain that in proposing a moral norm, the Church was truly interpreting the will of God. He concluded "this is why our response has been delayed and why it must be delayed for some time yet."

From these statements we can conclude that the matter was under consideration and that the norms of Pius XI and Pius XII were being questioned.

VATICAN II

In the meantime, Vatican II had issued its "Constitution on the Church and the Modern World" and in n.51 of this document, we read "there cannot be any true contradiction between the divine law regarding the transmission of new life and the fostering of true conjugal love." It continues "by virtue of these principles, the members of the Church are not permitted, in the regulation of procreation, to enter upon paths which are disapproved of by the Magisterium in its interpretation of divine law."

And in the footnotes reference is made to *Casti Connubii*, the Allocution to Nurses in 1951 and Pope Paul's promise of a thorough study of the problem in the light of new knowledge. The Council seemed to want to ratify the traditional doctrine but nothing in the text indicates that it went that far. One cannot say that the Council did anything definitive, particularly since the Pope had reserved the final decision to himself. The dissenters do not see at this point any solution to a probable doubt on the morality of contraception, at least on the part of the official magisterium in an authentic teaching. Was *Humanae Vitae* going to give the solution?

When *Humanae Vitae* issued, some theologians and philosophers commented on it but did not enter into the depths of the controversy. Thomas Gilkey O.P., of this group, thought the message was simply that human sexuality has a *social* aspect to it and is not an exclusive interpersonal relationship. This comes out nicely through the teaching of the *inseparability* of the unitive and procreative aspects of intercourse. This group saw no difficulty in accepting the doctrine, as long as it was agreed that the biological nature of the act specifies it morally, that humanity itself in its essential relationships is unchangeable and that Divine Providence will reward our trust and confidence in Him.

DISSENT

A group of theologians led by Charles Curran was pointed in its dissent on the premise that the physical structure of the act should *not* determine its morality. A panel of Belgian theologians (Heylen, Del Haye, Janssen) disagreed with the famous scripture scholar, Joseph Coppens, who urged the acceptance of the Encyclical despite the objection noted as to the basis of the morality of contraception.

He based his claim on the fact that the document represented the *traditional* teaching of the Church. (Heylen retorted that it was the constant

teaching because it was never subjected to any research effort all these years and was too dependent
upon one theory of body-function!)

Others accepted the Encyclical's view as to the
malice of contraception but desired to have this evil
tolerated in certain cases in order to promote a
greater good or avoid a worse evil. Their opinion
met with opposition, since contraception was de-
fined as intrinsically evil and thus could not be
made acceptable by dint of circumstances. They
replied that the evil in their estimation would not
be the *object* of the act of the will: it would be the
good sought from its toleration.

The philosopher, James Good, looked upon the
document as setting an ideal to be attained under
ideal conditions which could hardly be realized in
every day life. For him, it was another case of the
thesis versus the antithesis — what is ideal versus
what is really practicable.

A large group of theologians challenged the
basic contention of the Encyclical namely, "that
every act of matrimonial intercourse had to be open
to the transmission of new life." Those who had
held that the doctrine on contraception before
Humanae Vitae was in the state of probable doubt
were astonished that the Holy Father based his conclusion on the immorality of contraception on the
biological structure of the marital act.

Equally astonishing, for them, was the claim
that the doctrine was also that of the Natural Law.
They asked how the morality of an act could be
based on a physical trait, i.e., fertility — which in
fact does not occur that often. And to them this
raised the question: how moral is intercourse during
the infertile period?

Theological thought was favorable to taking the human person and his acts as the criterion of morality for actions. Even Vatican II had agreed that the moral character of any act should be taken from objective standards and mostly, from the nature of the human person and his acts.

The Papal Commission likewise had said that "the biological process in man is not some separated part of man but is integrated into the totality of his personality. Material fecundity in this process gets its moral value and meaning from the finalization toward the goods which define marriage." How could the Pope choose the physical structure of the act as a basis for its morality?

Furthermore, theologians noted that the arguments and analyses used in the authentic teaching from the Natural Law level did not support the conclusions of the Encyclical. It was contended that these arguments and analyses were inadequate, insufficient, questionable in value and not drawn from a wide-enough spectrum of 'what normal people choose when in such circumstances.'

The dissenters held to this opinion even though the Pope had made a special note that his teaching did not necessarily rest exclusively on the arguments adduced but also on the assistance of the Holy Spirit that is given to pastors of the Church to illustrate the truth. The theologians responded that this is true, but that the Holy Spirit must be aided by man and that His assistance does not relieve man from a diligent, adequate search of arguments and proofs to sustain non-infallible teaching. If such arguments are not solid and substantial, then the Holy Spirit cannot do His work. (cf Theological Studies: Sec. 1968, 725,743; Dec.1969, 656).

Added impetus was given to the dissenters by an article in the Irish Ecclesiastical Record to the effect that, just because there is a pattern for sex function, is not a sufficient reason to take such a pattern as the canon for human, moral behaviour. The writer believed that when the natural law is invoked in the area of morality, there is always an unfortunate mixture of the physical with the moral which trickles into a moral imperative.

Should man then be a slave to the physical structure of an act? Or should he be a free, responsible, moral agent able to modify the physical structure for a higher purpose? The generative faculty in man has a transcendental finality which supercedes the individual, personal finality of man's choice — but does this mean that such generative faculties are of an absolute inviolability in their inherent finality?

The article cited a Roman case in which three eminent theologians approved the use of the pill for a woman threatened by rape. This was equivalent to temporary *sterilization* yet it was approved. Seemingly, direct sterilization (evil in itself), is forbidden only when used for an evil end. Could not the same rule be applied in the use of the generative faculties of man?

A husband has rights to intercourse but not in an illimited manner. They must be used by him in a responsible human fashion. Why not apply the same theory to the physical structure of the act in contraception? It does not seem that it must always determine the morality of its use. The author went on to comment on the directives given by various bishops to their subjects on the fulfillment of *Humanae Vitae* in their own personal lives: did these confirm the *violability* of the norm that the physical nature of the act always calls for openness to the transmission of life? (cf Irish Ecclesiastical Record, April, 1967 p. 261)

John F. Kippley in 1971 contended that there was a way out of this dilemma. Since the tradition alleged is the work of the Spirit, should we not accept the presumed guidance of the Spirit and *agree* to accept *Humanae Vitae* on that score? True, we cannot prove by tangible methods the assistance of the Spirit in this document but neither can we prove the basis of the Encyclical by philosophical ethical norms.

He agreed that the Natural Law conclusions should be demonstrable to all men in order to have conclusive value and not just evident to believing Roman Catholics. But arguments from Natural Law are greatly handicapped for conclusive strength because of the modern, cultural background, the sinful environment and the atheistic and agnostic tendencies of our times. We have experienced this, he noted, not only on the birth control issue but more so on the abortion issue and of the two, the latter should have been as clear as day to any right-thinking man. In this dilemma, the only solution is to have recourse to the assistance of the Spirit given to the Church even in its non-infallible magisterium. (cf Theological Studies, March, 1971, p. 48)

PRACTICAL SUGGESTIONS

If there is such dissension in the ranks, which way do we turn in practice? Three attitudes present differing solutions.

One could be that the doctrine is as good as the arguments adduced: this would be *hostile* to papal authority and prerogative.

Another opinion could be that the teaching is true regardless of the arguments adduced: this would make the Pope *an arbitrary teacher* with no need of theological reflection even in non-infallible teaching: indeed a rash proposal.

The last opinion favors giving the *presumption of correctness* to the teaching by reason of religious docility of mind and will. But if an individual cannot bring himself to accept the conclusions, then it seems to me that the presumption prevails *until a sufficient number of mature and well-informed members of the community share the same difficulty and then the doctrine could be said to be doubtful.* This would apply only to non-infallible teaching. Only after the verification of these conditions can the question of norms binding in conscience be adequately answered.

Fr. Richard McCormick S.J. would claim that in the past decade a good number of theologians held that the traditional norms on contraception proposed by Pius XI and Pius XII were in genuine doubt and this for serious and positive reasons.

Humanae Vitae reaffirmed these norms relying on an unacceptable identification of the natural law with the material processes. For these theologians, the doctrine remains in the same status: doubtful.

It is worthy of remark that the claim that contraception is forbidden by the Natural Law was based on man's being as man. Ordinarily, a deduction from the Natural Law must come from many competencies, and its evidence must be available to everybody. In the case of contraception this prerequisite was not verified since even today so many challenge it. Many scholars believe that there seems to be no conclusive argument from Natural Law capable of sustaining the intrinsic malice of contraception. In fact, they claim that there is good evidence to the contrary.

Should we conclude that contraception then is a virtue? No. Oftentimes it will spring from a very materialistic and secularistic way of life. It may be infected with selfishness, infidelity and pre-marital irresponsibility. Through contraception there is a real danger that the true meaning and value of human sexuality may be lost.

When is it tolerable? "If the couple resolves to do its best to bring the fullness of the sexual act into their marital relationship . . . then the practice of contraception would not represent moral failure."

Are these opposition views erroneous? No, opposition to the Encyclical claims only that its doctrinal conclusions are open to solid, positive doubt since very strong objections can be urged against them and very little evidence sustains them.

In practice, what should be our attitude? In general, we must state without hesitation that the present non-infallible doctrine of the Papal Magisterium is that every contraceptive act is immoral.

What if a couple, after serious reflexion, dissents? Their views are to be respected. People should be encouraged to work for the ideal outlined by the Pope; and this in patience and with confidence in the grace of God. Should a couple so strive, and occasionally fall, they should not be held to be in serious sin.

The Holy Father wrote "if sin should still hold its sway over them, let them not be discouraged but rather have recourse with humble perseverance to the mercy of God. The Belgian Bishops did likewise when they wrote "such spouses are not to believe they are separated from God's love if they do not succeed immediately in adapting their behaviour to the norms of *Humanae Vitae*".

In the most recent pastoral of the American Episcopacy the bishops reaffirmed the teaching that contraception is wrong. But the amendment states that many couples face increasing pressures in family planning. Contraception can result from selfishness and improperly formed consciences, but also from conflicts and pressures which can mitigate culpability. (cf Trends Nov. 13, 1976.)

PART 4

PREMARITAL SEX

The custom of living together without a marriage certificate, is currently widespread. But, are those involved happy?

Recently, a free-lance writer had an interview with two honor students at a local university and this was the result: "My girl and I grooved together beautifully. We moved in with each other declaring that each was free to go his or her own way at any time.

"We had succumbed to the idea that absolute freedom provides the ultimate in an alliance. We felt that devotion to one another would be stronger than a signed document and that it might even tolerate a peccadillo now and then. But our life together was always in doubt.

"We would pool our money and buy a Porsch next year 'unless we are no longer around together'.

We would consider putting a down payment on a house 'if each of us is still around'. Our relationship became static without long term goals. A baby could not be considered. After the initial excitement wore off, lack of committal ties kept our relationship from being viable". (Theo Jackson Phi Beta Kappa student in "Marriage" Dec 1976 p. 23.)

Sexual liberty to the fullest extent is sought even by young adolescents as vital to their self-fulfillment. Depth psychology has inspired the development of sexual personalism; and this has been successful because of the decline of transcendental religion.

THE OLD VIEW

Classically, the argument against premarital sex ran as follows: the procreative characteristic of sex requires that the couple be in a permanent set of relationships in order to be able to assume the obligations owed to the potential progeny. This entails stability of their union and exclusive fidelity one to another.

Furthermore, the spouses were made very conscious of the social aspect of such obligations. It was unquestioned that the personal, human values of marriage and the social aspect of it were better served by a public, permanent institution and way of life. It was the family which was held to be the basic unit of society; and the one in which children were meant to be born and reared under the sign of a relationship of exclusive fidelity between God and man.

It was also taught that sex intimacy between the unmarried was a lie because there was no gift of self, no donation of bodies, and the quasi-communal life between the parties was a caricature of true, human, conjugal sexuality. Even if intercourse is contraceptive or sterile, its inherent character is belied and desecrated. The total gift of self which is part and parcel of marriage demands an irrevocable covenant of loving fidelity and the safeguard of a permanent bond and way of life.

NEW VIEWS

These norms are now questioned. Some would permit sex intimacy for those whose marriage would not be too remote in the future. Francis V Manning sees marriage as a *process*, and even though the ideal is intercourse reserved until marriage, individual weakness and pressures could well necessitate it once the couple has given its sincere intent to marry. Manning and Johannes Grundel figure that, really, marriage begins with the actual existence of true, marital consent and this sometimes precedes the public and legal ceremonies.

James Snoek sees three 'yes' stages: the 'yes' of the parties, the 'yes' of the Church and the 'yes' of the State along with the 'yes' of consummation. He wonders if the spouses could not for a good reason place consummation ahead of the other 'yes' stages?

Maurice Vidal would approve of premarital sex if the union was of the progressive type, i.e., if it really tended towards a publicly recognized union; he would refuse sex if the union was regressive, i.e., not at all tending this way.

Lester Kierhendall laments that campus-sex is of the regressive type because it is indulged in as an antidote for loneliness rather than as a pledge of loyalty, constancy and covenanted fidelity. Aptly he remarks — the language of sex is easy to speak but hard to make meaningful!

All authors agree that, as an ideal, full intimacy should be reserved for the married state. They agree that premarital sex exposes youth to a sort of sexual obsession and deprives it of all the superior values outlined in Christian traditions on marriage. Sex is the language of intimate relationship; and its full human meaning is best served by a covenanted love in the stability of a publicly-recognized way of life.

If marital love is going to be true to itself, and be generative, then it needs safeguards, and the qualities spoken of. If married love is going to bridge our loneliness and the isolation of our individuality, it must live in the promise of permanency. Then and then alone, will the sex experience be saved from collapse into a divisive, alienating, destructive trivialization.

It need hardly be said that views favoring premarital sex are still minority ones.

THE BIBLE

Intercourse between the unmarried is called *fornication* in biblical and theological language. The word "porneia" used in the Bible is a general term for unlawful, illicit sex. In particular it is used to mean sex outside of marriage. A recent writer contended that even if porneia (our pornography derivative) did not have the meaning of "fornication" in Paul, I Cor. 7 v.1-7, by all expert research it does mean what moderns politely name 'premarital sex'.

Paul gives no consolation to those who would justify this species of sex, for he writes "on account of fornication, let each man have his own wife, and each woman her own husband." And Paul tells the unmarried girl who does not have the gift that he, Paul, possesses, then, it were better that she marry lest fornication occur *"des tas porneias"* . . . and thus avoid the sins of sexual immorality.

In the Jerusalem Bible, chapter six, part D, the title is *Fornicatio*; and we read "keep away from fornication. All other sins are committed outside the body, but to fornicate is to sin against your own body." 6:18. In chapter 7 v. 9 "If they cannot control the sexual urges, they should get married, since it is better to be married, than to be tortured (by lust)." In chapter 5 Paul speaks of incest and in v 9-10, the Apostle tells his people that he would have them refrain from associating with people living immoral lives . . . but "I was not meaning to include all the people in the world who are sexually immoral . . . what I wrote was that you should not associate with a brother Christian who is leading an immoral life." (v 11.)

Christian tradition has always interpreted the sixth commandment in a broad sense to mean that sexual pleasure must not be taken outside the married state. It not only included adultery but all unchaste acts. Paul, in his epistle to the Corinthians, could not have been more explicit concerning the danger of sex misuse. (cf Premarital Sex: Theological studies, March, '73, 77; Sept. 1976, 478; Amer. Eccles. Review, 1971-'72.)

CONCLUSION

Where will all this sex permissiveness lead? Listen to a young divorcee: "I stayed with Bob for the usual reason. I felt that my children needed a father. But there could be no emotional attachment to a man who saw every female as a potential bed partner. Bob's need to prove himself as a super stud eventually affected the way he dealt with all of us so I ended by having no qualms about ending our tenuous relationship." (MARRIAGE, p. 23, Dec. 1976.)

Dr. J. D. Unwin has been quoted as saying "any human society is free to choose either to display great energy, or to enjoy sexual freedom; the evidence is that it cannot do both for more than one generation."

Dr. Bethlehem says "It is simply not true that sex is no longer surrounded by anxieties; or that sex no longer leads to serious difficulties . . . public morality, unfortunately, has failed to be concerned with the damage people may inflict on themselves or on each other." (MARRIAGE, Dec. 1976, p. 23.)

The loving, indepth relationship between man and woman enhances the personalities of both participants; promiscuity can lead to neurosis and instability and even to disease.

Dr. Bender, M.D., in his "In Necessity and Sorrow" (cf Miami Herald, Tropic Magazine section Nov 21, 1976) is quoted as saying that "I've had the quest of extra-marital sex come up in my practice and I've spoken to women about it . . . we are not that liberated . . . the relationship is being sought, I feel sadly, through a sex contact, and I think this has to reduce one's self respect. I feel that it takes a significant and meaningful aspect of one's life out of context. I think that we are certainly living in a time of decreased human respect, of decreased human relationships and of decreased aversion to killing off things. If you lose that importance or significance of sex you just in another way evade another means of humanistic response and we have lost enough of that!"

Someone has aptly remarked that Pope Paul VI may have been terribly chagrined by the response to his *Humanae Vitae* but that, when history is written, Paul may stand out like His namesake and that *we* may be chagrined for not having heard his call for greater reverence, integrity and humanity in the realm of sex and conjugal loving relationships! (cf Nancy Cox: Have we been duped about sex? in MARRIAGE, Dec. '76 21-24.)

The American bishops in their 1976 Pastoral aptly comment "Our society gives considerable encouragement to premarital and extramarital sexual relations as long as 'no one gets hurt'. Such relations are not worthy of beings created in God's image, and made God's adopted children, nor are they according to God's Will (I Cor. 6:9-10,18).

The unconditional love of Christian marriage is absent, for such relations are hedged around by many conditions. Though tenderness and concern may sometimes be present, there is an underlying tendency toward exploitation and self-deception. Such relations trivialize sexuality and can erode the possiblity of making deep, lifelong, commitments."

FOOTNOTES

HOMOSEXUALITY

1. Cavanagh, Dr. J. R. Latent Homosexuality as a Cause of Marital Discord (Linacre Quarterly, Aug. '76, 139).
2. Buckley, Rev. M. J. Morality and the Homosexual, Newman, 1960.
3. Buckley, 83
4. Idem, 101

Judeo-Christian Viewpoint:
1. Vatican Declaration on Sexual Ethics, Origins, Jan. 22, '76

Medical Viewpoint:
1. Farnsworth-Braceland: Psychiatry, the Clergy and Pastoral Counseling, Collegeville, Minn. 1969, 268.
2. PASTORAL LIFE, March, '74, Canfield, Ohio.
3. Buckley, cited, 138

Moral Viewpoint:
1. Bishops' Committee on Pastoral Research, March, '74 — Principles to guide Confessors on Questions of Homosexuality.

Legal Viewpoint:
1. Elbert, E. J. I Understand, Sheed & Ward, 1971, 149

Other Viewpoints:
1. Harvey, J. F. A Critique of John McNeill, sj/Gregory Baum (in Linacre Quarterly, Aug. '76, 196)
2. Curran, Chas. E. Sexual Ethics; Reaction to a Critique in Linacre Quarterly, Aug. '76, 196)

ABORTION
1. PASTORAL LIFE, April, '76: Abortion, it is Human, C. E. Miller
   What it is:
1. Theological Studies, June, '76: Abortion, Biological Considerations
   D. Granfield, The Abortion Decision, Doubleday, 1969, P. 27
   Chicago Studies, Fall, '71, 314

Judeo-Christian Viewpoint:
1. Callahan: Abortion, the Law, etc., 410
2. Vatican Declaration on Abortion in Origins, Dec. 12, '74, 387
3. Theological Studies, Sept. 1970, 495

Medical Viewpoint:
1. Theological Studies, Sept. '73, N. 3, P. 481
2. Callahan, cited, 59
3. idem, 72
4. idem, 80

Moral Viewpoint:
1. Catholic Mind, May 1972, 49-52
   Idem Archbishop Whealon, 43
   Chicago Studies, 1972, 305-312
   Idem, 298

Legal Viewpoint:
1. Origins, Oct. 2, 1975 Human Life Amendment
   PASTORAL LIFE, Jan. 1976
2. Origins, Dec. 12, '74: Vatican Declaration
3. Hartford Transcript, Aug. 27, 1976
4. Origins, July 15, '76: Supreme Court Rules etc.
5. Views from Congress, Origins, April 1, '74

Other Viewpoints:
1. PASTORAL LIFE, Oct. '72, 39
   Chicago Studies Fall, '71, 331
2. PASTORAL LIFE, Oct. '72, 40;
   Chicago Studies, 327
3. Callahan, cited, 378-390
4. Views from Congress, Origins, April 1, '74
5. PASTORAL LIFE, Aug. '74, 13, How Far Can We Go in Human
   Experimentation? Geo. Kanoti, Ph.D.
6. Origins, June 12, '75, Toward a Policy in Fetal Research
   PASTORAL LIFE, May 1974, Genetic Counseling (P. Gastonguay)

ANOTHER FINE BOOK

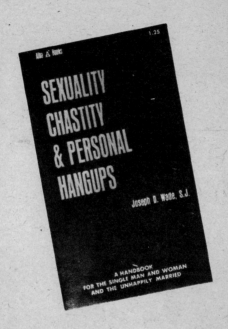

SEXUALITY, CHASTITY AND PERSONAL HANGUPS by Joseph D. Wade — Fr. Wade has more than 30 years' counselling experience and he draws on this rich source to give help with guilt feelings and scruples in the sexual area and to offer guidance and comfort to all celibates: priests, religious and lay people.

— $1.25

BATTERED WIVES: The Secret Scandal by Harold J. Pascal, C.M. — Wife-beating is recognized as a near universal problem, but cultural conditioning, the application of the law, the criminal justice system and personal biases have kept the tragic facts out of sight.

Some time-honored myths about wife-beating are exploded in this book. What obstacles does an abused wife face in attempting to win elementary justice for herself? What is the murky motivation behind the husband and his behavior? Why does the woman often continue to remain in this self-defeating situation?

You will find the answer to most of your questions in this comprehensive, socio-psychological treatment of a painful subject. It is not a mere litany of ills but instead proposes pratical and feasible remedies to bring relief to millions of silent sufferers.

$1.75

1.65

Tell Me Again You Love Me

JOHN C. TORMEY

TELL ME AGAIN YOU LOVE ME by John C. Tormey — Here is delightful reading about the majority vocation, marriage. Illustrated with cartoons for today's young people, it has an equally-meaningful message for their parents.

$1.65

Are there ALBA BOOKS titles you want but cannot find in your local stores? Simply send name of book and retail price plus 60¢ to cover mailing and handling costs to:

ALBA BOOKS, Canfield, Ohio, 44406.